3rd Edition

The

A B

of

Collecting Online

by Ray Boileau

Published by

Hobby House Press
Grantsville, Maryland 21536
www.hobbyhouse.com

DEDICATION

To Carolyn, my best find of all.

ABC's of Collecting Online has been written to be as accurate as possible. The author, publisher, agents and assignees cannot be held responsible for any error that may occur within the text of this book, nor held responsible for any problems or computer viruses that the user may encounter utilizing the Internet or any other online service provider.

Photo - Title Page: An ornate carved wooden jewelry box with mirror.

Additional copies of this book may be purchased at $12.95 (plus postage and handling)
from
Hobby House Press, Inc.
1 Corporate Drive
Grantsville, Maryland 21536
1-800-554-1447
or from your favorite bookstore or dealer.
©2000 by Ray Boileau

ISBN: 0-87588-583-7

TABLE OF CONTENTS

INTRODUCTION

Having crossed into a new century that seems destined to be technology driven, the significance of our past is amplified with each day that passes. The speed with which the world moves today has made us all, at one time or another, think about what we perceive as "simpler times." Baby boomers yearn for the toys of their youth. Doll collectors yearn for the Bru that twenty years ago they could afford and now cannot. Furniture enthusiasts bemoan the fact that the oldest and best examples have found their way into museums and private collections, and have all but disappeared from the marketplace. What's left to collect?

Everything and anything! Most of us have a natural instinct to collect, and share an unexplained desire to amass "stuff." For others, the thrill of the hunt is the most desirable part of collecting; finding, purchasing and owning the item is actually secondary and in some cases a letdown. If you identify with this type, consider that you may enjoy being a dealer more than a collector. Perhaps your grandmother gave you a piece of depression glass, as mine did years ago, and after some study you discovered that there were many more pieces in her pattern available. I now have an extensive collection of yellow Florentine #2 depression glass because it reminds me of someone I respected, admired, and miss greatly.

Nostalgia plays a big part in collecting for many of us, and the 1950s–1970s are hot decades for collectibles. Why? Many of us born in the 1950s are now entering our peak earnings years and have more disposable income available to buy back our childhoods. Maybe you started off to school each day with your Roy Rogers lunchbox and, in inclement weather, your Roy Rogers rain slicker. Wouldn't it be fun to own them again?

Those born in the 1960s and 1970s have grown up during the computer revolution and want to in some small way hold on to a time before everything doubled in speed every five years. They don't remember Gene Autry or Tom Mix but do remember Quark cereal and Charlie's Angels.

Your collecting fancy doesn't even have to be for older things. Beanie Babies and Pokémon are perfect examples of collectibles introduced quite recently that have gained immediate popularity. The *Gene*® doll, introduced in 1995 by Ashton-Drake, has captured the imagination of doll collectors who want to play with their dolls as well as opened doors for other collectible dolls like *Tyler Wentworth* by The Robert Tonner Doll Company. There is already a secondary market for these recently introduced collectibles, with some items selling for hundreds and even thousands of dollars more than they cost just a few years ago.

That being said, I urge you to not get caught up in the "collecting for profit" trap unless you're a dealer and at least some of your livelihood comes from buying and selling. Otherwise, treat the buying and selling of antiques and collectibles as a hobby—if you make a few bucks at it great, but don't count on it paying the bills. For every story of somebody paying $25.00 for a piece of Roseville pottery in the morning and selling it for $250.00 that same afternoon, there are thousands of disappointing stories you won't hear.

Even experienced dealers don't always get it right when buying for profit. In fact, I can assure you that every full-time dealer has more stories than they would like to remember about merchandise they paid too much for and then couldn't resell to break even. I have an inventory book full of "bargains" I have listed on the Internet without a reserve—so sure they would sell for much more than I paid and so disappointed when they didn't. Collecting for pleasure is much less painful!

Market conditions have changed radically since eBay™ opened its virtual doors in late 1995. Until then collections were built over time, and amassing a sizeable collection required visiting antique malls, flea markets, yard sales, auctions…in short, logging a lot of miles. Most collectors didn't have the time or money it required to travel the entire country searching for that one elusive piece, and settled for buying trips within a few hours drive from home.

Today, the Internet has opened a vast market that you can access from your living room, basement, even the local library. Collections that used to take a lifetime to acquire can now be completed in a few weeks, if you're willing and able to spend the money that quickly. The rules have changed, and you need to change with them to take full advantage of the possibilities.

For some time, eBay™ was the only game in town. Now there are hundreds of Internet auction sites, but none has so much as dented eBay™'s dominance of the marketplace. Several sites that launched during the past few years have already expired in 2000, and most of the survivors do not seem to be flourishing.

Amazon.com was expected to give eBay™ a run for their money when they launched their auction business. Although Amazon.com has made a strong showing compared to others, so far it is not a serious challenger. All of this is somewhat disturbing, as the Internet has been touted as a way for small business to achieve equal footing with the big boys. In the world of online auctions, this has not yet proven to be true—if Amazon.com can't challenge eBay™ what chance does anybody else have?

The popularity and success of online auctions has created opportunities for another type of business—online auction tools. You can use software tools to create eye-catching auction ads, add counters to keep track of how many visitors look at your auction or page, bid for you when you're away from your computer, search for the best deals among several sites, and even transfer funds to anyone with an e-mail address. A seller profiled in my book *The ABCs of Making Money Online* was contacted by one such business, *AuctionRover.com,* and went to work for them as one of their experts. He never envisioned that simply using the online auctions could lead to a job with a new Web-based company catering to the needs of other online auction users. Such is the way of the new economy.

Since you're reading this book, you've probably already got the collecting bug. If you don't have it, keep reading and then experience the online auctions. I'm betting you'll be hooked. We all like to collect something—even your house collects dust!

A Department 56 Christmas House, "Turn of the Century House," from 1984.

Child's play dishes; teapot is stamped "Mickey Mouse//copp (sic) by// Walt Disney//Made in Japan."

Three snow globes from the 1st limited edition New England Collectors Society Disney series.

A tapestry showing an aerial view of the 1933/34 Chicago World's Fair, known as "The Century of Progress Fair."

Guidebook to the 1933/34 Chicago World's Fair.

CHAPTER 1
WELCOME TO THE FUTURE!

The Internet is here to stay, and the faster you get on board the better. Not only that, it is maturing at an alarming rate. Most retailers racked up Internet sales well exceeding their projections during the 1999 Christmas season as America rushed to capitalize on the ease of shopping online. Picture first getting up early Saturday morning, getting dressed, driving through holiday traffic to the local mall, fighting crowds in store after store and not finding the right gifts, dragging uncle Paul's new TV to the car, and finally coming home hungry and tired only to realize you forgot aunt Gladys and have to go out again. Wouldn't you rather sleep in Saturday morning, turn on your computer (when you finally decide to get up), browse huge inventories of gifts in the privacy of your own home while in your pajamas, and have your purchases shipped to your doorstep? Or stay up late Friday night and get your shopping done while you're watching a Ray Harryhausen sci-fi classic—the Internet stores don't close. It's not hard to understand the allure.

To have access to this powerful medium you need only a computer with a keyboard and monitor, a modem, browser software (both of these items are typically provided with new computer purchases), a phone line, and a willingness to learn. In this new century even Internet access can be free, and paying a monthly fee to an Internet Service Provider is no longer necessary if you're willing to view advertisements at the top of your computer screen while you're online. When these conditions are satisfied you become one of millions of computers networked to the World Wide Web, thus forming the Internet. Once there you will marvel at the ease of navigation provided by hyperlinks and search engines. You will be astounded at the sheer volume of antiques and collectibles that are suddenly available for purchase, and you will become a member of a global community. Your life will be changed forever.

The U.S. military originally conceived what today is known as the Internet as a way of keeping communications open in time of national emergency. In the late 1960s the Defense Department commissioned the Advanced Research Projects Agency (ARPA) to devise a system of communications, using computers, that could be rerouted in the event that main lines were destroyed or tampered with. This network came to be known as ARPANET and, in the beginning, was difficult to use in contrast to today's user-friendliness.

Next to recognize the importance of interconnected domains was the academic community. In searching for a way to quickly distribute information among themselves and their universities, the National Science Foundation began forming their own network, which was dubbed NSFNET in its honor. NSFNET was built during the 1980s and eventually connected with the military network, with the result being the beginnings of the Internet we know today.

Internet Access

The route most people take to the Internet is their home telephone line. Other avenues are available, such as access over cable TV lines, ISDN or T-1 lines, and satellite connections. These other types of Internet access provide faster throughput of data but are more expensive than using existing phone lines. The average user, including home office workers and small businesses, can get by readily with a phone line connection. The casual user may want to investigate WebTV, which utilizes a VCR-like box that sits on top of your television set and affords you Internet access via your TV screen. This is the least expensive way to get to the Internet, but is also the most limiting in terms of visual resolution. You need a keyboard with WebTV if you want to interact; otherwise you can only watch as the Internet passes you by.

Your Window to the World

Computer users need software aptly called a browser to open the window and let the Internet in. Netscape Navigator and Microsoft's Internet Explorer are the two most commonly used. Both browsers are good, and I don't recommend one over the other. You'll probably end up using the one a friend recommends, the one that is already installed on your computer, or the one that you get your hands on first. Browsers are started, or launched, the same way most other programs on your computer are, from the Start—Programs menu if you are using Windows 95 or 98, or from a shortcut icon on your desktop.

Addresses

Once your window to the world is open, how do *you point your browser* where you want it to go? By using an address, known in Internet

10

lingo as a URL (Uniform Resource Locator). Every resource on the World Wide Web has its own unique URL. URL is pronounced one letter at a time just as you see it: U-R-L. If you refer to it by pronouncing a word that rhymes with girl you will be identifying yourself as a novice, and we wouldn't want that, would we?

The majority of documents you view online are created in *hypertext markup language* (html), currently the standard language of the Internet. This language allows the linking abilities that make navigating the Internet so interesting. By simply clicking on a hypertext link you are whisked to another part of the document you are viewing, or perhaps to a completely new document, which contains further information about the link you just clicked on.

Most Internet addresses take the form ***http://www.servername.xxx*** where http:// stands for *hypertext transfer protocol* (note that the :// after http MUST be used and the slashes must be the forward, and not backward, slashes), www stands for *world wide web*, servername is the name an Internet Service Provider uses to identify their host computer, and xxx is an abbreviation for the type of *domain* the address is using. The different parts are separated by a period, pronounced "dot" when reciting the address. Abbreviations for U.S. domains are as follows...

com	Business and Commercial
edu	Educational Institutions
gov	Government Institutions
mil	Military Installations
net	Network Resources
org	Other organizations

Web Sites and Web Pages

A Web page can be as simple as a paragraph of text or as complex as a combination of text, animated graphics, and audio and video clips. Most Web pages have hyperlinks, which appear as different colored and/or underlined text, or sometimes as a colored box around a graphic. When you pass your cursor over a hyperlink the arrow changes to a hand with a finger pointing up. When you click on a hyperlink you are whisked to a different part of the Web page you are viewing or possibly to another Web page entirely. A group of Web pages that are designed to be viewed together, one at a time, using hyperlinks, is called a *Web site.*

Search Engines

The fastest way to find Web sites related to a particular topic is by using a *search engine*. A search engine allows you to type in a word or words, known as *keywords*, that you are seeking information about and it then "searches" the Internet for Web sites that contain those words. What actually happens is that the search engines are constantly monitoring the Internet with programs referred to as robots. Information is collected and indexed in database form, readily available to answer inquiries. Otherwise a search of the Internet would take much longer than any of us is willing to wait.

There are options for narrowing your search if the engine returns too many sites (which it often does) or you can run a new search adding or omitting some of your keywords. The search engine will return a page or pages of hyperlinks with brief descriptions of the Web site that you simply click on to go to that site.

Be aware that all search engines are not created equal; that's one reason there is more than one of them. Each search engine provider hopes that their product will be the most comprehensive at finding quality Web sites to match your search parameters. Realistically the World Wide Web is a huge place and the technology available today just doesn't allow a single search engine to find everything—it is estimated that even the best search engines are capable of indexing less than 20% of the entire Internet. Therefore, should you not find any matches for your search with, say, the *AltaVista*™ search engine, try *Yahoo!*, *Webcrawler*™ and several others before abandoning your quest.

You can type more than one word when using a search engine and it will search for Web sites containing any of the words. If you want to search for a string of words that must fall together exactly as you type them, enclose them in quotes. For example, a search of the AltaVista™ search engine yielded the following results...

A search for the word **dolls** returned 488,921 sites.

A search for the words **modern dolls**, without quotes, returned 797,830 sites. In this case the search engine is looking for sites that contain either of the keywords anywhere on the site.

A search for the words **"modern dolls"**, with quotes, returned 771 sites, because the search found only sites that used the keywords in the exact order they were typed.

In contrast, here are the results of the same searches on the Webcrawler™ search engine...

A search for the word **dolls** returned 5273 sites.

A search for the words **modern dolls**, without quotes, returned 36,529 sites.

A search for the words **"modern dolls"**, with quotes, returned 26 sites.

As mentioned before, it is good to get familiar with several search engines, as they will return different results. In our example above, AltaVista™ returned many more sites, in fact too many to explore without narrowing the field. Statistics show that most people will look no further than the first 10 entries returned by a search engine before moving on. Even with all of those choices, you might find the exact site you are looking for in the Webcrawler™ results instead, so remember to explore when your first search comes up empty!

If a search engine returns hyperlinks with a percentage in front of each one, that percentage represents how much of your search string was found on that particular page. Obviously you should visit the highest percentage pages first. To help get you started, here are the URLs of my favorite search engines. Once you get the hang of using them you can use these search engines to search for other search engines!

www.altavista.digital.com
www.excite.com
www.hotbot.com
www.infoseek.com
www.lycos.com
www.northernlight.com
www.webcrawler.com
www.yahoo.com

When you visit these search engine sites, I would recommend that you *bookmark* them for future use. Bookmarking is simply adding them to the *Favorites* menu of your browser, allowing you to return to the site with a single click from that point on.

Your browser will probably have both a menu and a toolbar button for Favorites—they perform similar functions. The menu categories go across the very top of the browser window, and the toolbar buttons are below it.

Go to the **Favorites** menu of your browser and click **Add To Favorites**. Depending on which browser you use, and which operating system resides on your computer, you will get a message asking if you want to subscribe to the page or something similar. Windows 98 users will simply get a dialog box saying that Internet Explorer will add the page to your favorites list. If you get the message asking if you want to subscribe to a page select **No, Just Add to Favorites** and then click **OK**. Windows 98 users can simply click **OK**. Note also that you can arrange your favorites into folders for easy access later. For instance, you can create a folder for search engines and one for online auctions so you don't have to look through sites for both when wanting to visit again.

From that point on, by clicking the Favorites button on the toolbar you will see a list of sites you have bookmarked. If you organize your favorite sites into folders you will see the folders and must click on the appropriate one to open it. Click once on any of the sites to be taken there immediately. If you're having problems or want to learn more, go to the Search feature of your browser's Help menu and type in the word favorite for additional information.

Netiquette

I would be remiss if I didn't mention something about the way to conduct yourself when online. There are a few "rules of the Internet highway" that you should know before communicating with the world.

1. Always remember you are a member of a community, and are responsible for your actions and particularly your words. Whether conversing via e-mail, posting an online auction listing or posting to a news group you must never forget that you are interacting with people, not computers. People have emotions, so pay attention to your message.

2. Don't use capital letters when communicating via the Internet—it's considered the online equivalent of yelling.

3. Keep it brief! Verbosity will only bore and possibly anger the Internet community. Most Internet surfers are in a hurry and aren't online to read *War and Peace*.

4. When responding to someone else's message, quote what they said along with your answer. Many e-mail programs allow you to do this

automatically—read the **Help** file of your program to see how to set the default to send messages with your replies.

5. Always remember that your private e-mail is not entirely private. It is possible for your messages to be intercepted by others, so you should never send private information (credit card numbers, etc.) unless you are on a secure server (if your URL address window says https:// instead of http:// and/or if your browser toolbar shows a locked padlock you're secure) or without first learning about the encryption features of your e-mail program. Go to the **Help** menu of your e-mail program and search for the word **encrypt**. After reading and understanding the information, you can make an informed decision about whether you trust sending sensitive information this way. It is also a good policy to send credit card information in two separate e-mail messages, with each message containing one-half of the number. This practice greatly reduces the chance of someone being able to intercept it.

A tiny vaporizer with the original box.

15

SEARCH ENGINES

www.altavista.com

Search   **Advanced Search**   **Images**   **MP3/Audio**   **Video**

Find this: [   ] [Search] [any language ▼]

• Help
• Family Filter is **off**
• Language Settings

Example: **+hotels +Paris -"bed and breakfast"**

Find Results on: ⦿ The Web ○ News ○ Discussion Groups ○ Products 2 pts *new!*

Rewards *new!* Money Sports Women Health Travel Real Estate News Jobs Translate Entertainment Chats

My Live! **Law** Message Boards Free Internet Access Radio Email Yellow Pages People Finder Directions Tech

Breaking News

• Wendy's Suspect Was a Fugitive
• FBI Pursues Cause of New Virus
• Hockey Legend Richard Dies
• Mexico Launches Web Portal
• Rats! How Contestants Survive

What's On AltaVista Now

Music: For love or money?

Tune in: 150 channels on AltaVista Radio

'Survivor': Yummy rats
Rewards: **Daily winners!**
'M:i-2': Packs theaters
Create: **Homepages**
Photos: **Memorial Day**

freeIM.org -- Fight the IM lockout

Fast Find:
Yellow Pages | Directions
Stock Quotes | Go Wireless
FOXSPORTS.COM Video

AltaVista Business Solutions

• Try AltaVista Search Engine 3.0
• License AltaVista Search

• Add a URL
• Raging Search *new!*
• Advanced Text Only
• Make AltaVista my Home Page
• Join the Affiliate Network: Earn Cash

AltaVista Directory: The Web's Largest

Arts & Entertainment
Movies, TV, Music...

Autos
Classic, Dealers, Manufacturers...

Business & Finance
Industries, Jobs, Investing...

Computers
Software, Hardware, Graphics...

Games
Video, Role-Playing, Gambling...

Health & Fitness
Conditions, Medicine, Alternative...

Home & Family
Kids, Houses, Consumers...

Internet
Chat, Email, WWW...

News & Media
Online, Magazines, Newspapers...

Recreation & Travel
Food, Outdoors, Humor...

Reference
Maps, Education, Libraries...

Regions & Languages
World, US, Europe...

Science
Biology, Psychology, Physics...

Shopping 1 pt
Web-Wide Auction, Compare, WWW Sites...

Society & Culture
People, Religion, Issues...

Sports
Baseball, Soccer, Football...

Hot Searches

Top **Bands** Searched for in MP3/Audio:

1. Korn
2. Limp Bizkit
3. Metallica

4. Depeche Mode
5. Smashing Pumpkins
6. Beasty Boys

AltaVista Search Guides: Find what you are looking for!

Buy a House
Invest Online
Buy a Car

Health Issues
Find a University
more guides...

Shopping Rewards *new!*

Win a Mercedes!
Autobahn experience - complete with SLK230 and trip to Germany more...

Top Rewards
• Register 1500 pts
• Hot Deals 50 pts
• More Top Rewards...

Win Prizes!
• Win instantly
• Tour France's finest vineyards
• Explore the heart of Africa

Deals & Auctions
• Web-Wide AuctionWatch
• Bargain Auction
• Find Hot Deals

Featured Sponsors

• Shop by request at Respond.com!
• For Yellow Page information visit WorldPages
• ShoppingList.com Search Local Sales
• Find a new job with AltaVista Careers!

Välkommen till AltaVista!

AltaVista in:
• France
• Germany
• Italy
• Sweden
• Netherlands
• UK
• Other...

Translate

www.excite.com

Welcome Ray!

Sign Out · Page Settings · Member Services · Help

Choose your favorite photo! »

My Excite
✉ **Check Voicemail/Email**
📖 **Calendar/Address Book**

Content · Layout · Color

Today On Excite
Saturday, May 27, 8:17PM
News Crayon Health Hazard?
  Poll Open Adoptions?
- Blind Date Personals
- Exotic Car Photos
- Hot! Win $10,000!

Win a flight to college

[Search] More

Autos	Entertainment	Lifestyle
Business	Family	Real Estate
Careers	Games	Relationships
Computers	Health	Sports
Education	Investing	Travel

Thousands of Photos for Your Desktop

Shopping Classifieds Auctions Gift Zone Bikinis and More
Gadget Guru

[**People & Chat**] Chat! 9671 People Meet People
ZinK Teens Find Friends Voice Chat More...

Shortcuts
Today's News
Free E-Cards
Stock Quotes
Yellow Pages
Free Web Access
Concert/Event Tickets Hot!
Photo Screen Savers
Classifieds
Maps & Directions
Horoscopes
More...

edit _ X

My Stocks
Portfolio Sponsored By
Charles Schwab OPEN ACCOUNT TRADE NOW

Full Portfolio | Stock News

Symbol	Price	Change
Nasdaq	3205.11	-0.24
Dow	10299.24	0.00
S&P 500	1378.02	-3.50
ATHM	17.69	-0.61
INTU	33.31	+1.38

Open an account with Schwab

Get Quotes: [   ] [Go]
Find Symbol
Most Active | Get Alerts

* = News Today
H/L = 52 wk high/low
Last update May 26 5:16PM
Data delayed at least 20 minutes

My News
Top Stories | Photos (May 27 7:10PM)
- Ulster Unionists Back Power Share
- Israel Troops Leave Lebanon Outpost
- Wendy's Suspect Was a Fugitive

ZDNet Tech News (May 26 9:20AM)
- Movie sites gear up for holiday weekend
- Linux losing its buzz on Wall Street
- Alpha chip update -- it ain't dead yet

Business News (May 27 5:05PM)
- Dow Ends Down 25; Nasdaq Off 0.24
- FBI Pursues Cause of E-mail Virus
- Pa. AG Probes United-US Air Deal

Sports News (May 27 7:32PM)
- Knicks Overcome Injuries to Beat Pacers in Game 3
- Woods Leads Memorial by Six Shots
- Canadian Hockey Legend Richard Dies at 78

Oddly Enough News (May 26 1:10PM)
- Inmate Auctions Execution Seats on eBay
- Hijacker Found Dead; Homemade Chute Failed
- Woman Dies After Being Bitten by Ants

NewsTracker Clipping Service
- Create your own personalized news topics

More News...

www.hotbot.com

www.infoseek.com

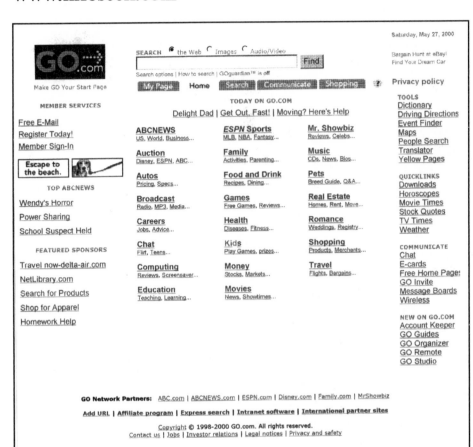

SEARCH ● the Web ○ Images ○ Audio/Video

Find

Search options | How to search | GOguardian™ is off

Make GO Your Start Page

My Page   Home   Search   Communicate   Shopping   ?

Bargain Hunt at eBay!
Find Your Dream Car

Privacy policy

MEMBER SERVICES

Free E-Mail
Register Today!
Member Sign-In

Escape to the beach.

TOP ABCNEWS

Wendy's Horror
Power Sharing
School Suspect Held

FEATURED SPONSORS

Travel now-delta-air.com
NetLibrary.com
Search for Products
Shop for Apparel
Homework Help

TODAY ON GO.COM

Delight Dad | Get Out, Fast! | Moving? Here's Help

ABCNEWS
US, World, Business...

Auction
Disney, ESPN, ABC...

Autos
Pricing, Specs...

Broadcast
Radio, MP3, Media...

Careers
Jobs, Advice...

Chat
Flirt, Teens...

Computing
Reviews, Screensaver...

Education
Teaching, Learning...

ESPN Sports
MLB, NBA, Fantasy...

Family
Activities, Parenting...

Food and Drink
Recipes, Dining...

Games
Free Games, Reviews...

Health
Diseases, Fitness...

Kids
Play Games, prizes...

Money
Stocks, Markets...

Movies
News, Showtimes...

Mr. Showbiz
Reviews, Celebs...

Music
CDs, News, Bios...

Pets
Breed Guide, Q&A...

Real Estate
Homes, Rent, Move...

Romance
Weddings, Registry...

Shopping
Products, Merchants...

Travel
Flights, Bargains...

TOOLS
Dictionary
Driving Directions
Event Finder
Maps
People Search
Translator
Yellow Pages

QUICKLINKS
Downloads
Horoscopes
Movie Times
Stock Quotes
TV Times
Weather

COMMUNICATE
Chat
E-cards
Free Home Pages
GO Invite
Message Boards
Wireless

NEW ON GO.COM
Account Keeper
GO Guides
GO Organizer
GO Remote
GO Studio

GO Network Partners: ABC.com | ABCNEWS.com | ESPN.com | Disney.com | Family.com | MrShowbiz

Add URL | Affiliate program | Express search | Intranet software | International partner sites

19

www.lycos.com

Free ISP - Find it - Talk about it - Shop for it

Search for [   ] **Go Get It!** ®

Advanced Search | Multimedia | Parental Controls

Topics Shop Autos Computers Entertainment Finance Games Health Kids **Music** Small Biz Sports Travel
Find Auctions Books Chat Clubs Ecards Email Free ISP **MP3** Maps People Stocks Yellow Pages **More**...

Lycos News   Edit
May 27, 2000

Bid Now & Win $10,000 from Lycos Auctions

More events...

- U.N. Troops Block Lebanon-Israel Border
- First U.S. Federal Execution in 37 Years
- **POLL** - U.S. Gun Laws: Keep 'Em/Ditch 'Em?

More News...

My Lycos - Personalize
Sign up, Log in...

San Francisco, CA
Partly Cloudy, **61°F**
Change to your city

Arts & Entertainment
Music, Celebrities, Movies...

Recreation
Food, Outdoors, Humor...

Lycos Shop
Browse Categories

- Clothing
- Computers
- Electronics
- Gifts & Occasions
- Home & Garden
- Toys & Games

More...

Featured

- Graduation gifts
- Prom Fashions
- Bid to Win $10,000
- Buy books for dad
- Computer Auctions

Autos
Buying, Parts, Repairs...

Reference
Education, Maps, Databases...

Business & Careers
Jobs, Investing, Real Estate...

Regional
US, Europe, Asia...

Computers & Internet
Software, Internet, Hardware...

Science & Technology
Biology, Astronomy, Earth...

Games
Card, Computer, Arcade...

Society & Culture
Relationships, People, Women...

Health
Diseases, Women, Medicine...

Sports
Baseball, College, Basketball...

News
Newspapers, Weather, Breaking...

Travel
Lodging, Destinations, Air Travel...

The Future is Here! Lycos TV

More: Banking Calendar College Home & Family Home Pages Horoscopes
Instant Messenger Lycos 50 Message Boards Pictures

¿Hablas español? ¡Echa un vistazo a Terra.com, nuestro nuevo socio!

Europe: Belgium, Denmark, France, Germany, Italy, Netherlands, Norway, Spain, Sweden, Switzerland, UK
Asia Pacific: China, Hong Kong, Japan, Korea, Malaysia, Singapore, Taiwan
Americas: Estados Unidos, Argentina, Brazil, Chile, Colombia, Mexico, Peru, Venezuela

Help - About Us - Advertise - Feedback - Jobs - Lycos MasterCard
Add Your Site to Lycos - Affiliate Program - Lycos Search for Missing Children

www.northernlight.com

Northern Light

NORTHERN LIGHT CUSTOM SEARCH FORMS

Simple Search   **Power Search**   Search News   Special Editions™
Business Search   Investext Search   Stock Quotes   Geo Search

Be specific: Instead of **turkey**, use **turkey recipes**.

Search for [_____] **Search**   Tips

Select a source [Search all Northern Light Sources ▾]

Did You Know ???

Special Editions™

Concise information on important
issues such as E-Commerce and
the 106th Congress. We can craft
custom Special Editions for
your organization.

- Find out more.
- See our current Special Editions.

B2B Business to Business

Northern Light has the content, technology,
and expertise to provide a solution to all
your company's information management
needs:

Visit NLResearch.com, our enterprise search site
Helping businesses and information work together
Find out about our Enterprise Accounts
Arrange for a demonstration or presentation
Read about some of our current partners

Search Alert Service

Free personalized news and research email
updates covering the topics of your choice.
Learn more.

Intelligent Searching

Northern Light has comprehensive search
features to enable you to save time while
finding exactly what you need.

Huge web database   Advanced Search Techniques
Helpful search forms   What is Special Collection?
Fewer dead links   Natural Language Search

Dow Jones Industrials	10297.53	-26.39

Updated May 26, 2000 02:33 PM EDT   Get A Stock Quote

Today's Headlines   More headlines ...

Maurice 'The Rocket' Richard Dies
Wendy's Suspect Was a Fugitive
Knicks 98, Pacers 95
Gore Criticizes Bush Nuclear Plan
Sierra Leone Rebels, Gov't Clash

News stories updated continuously

Search Listen and Win!

Live in Austin, Denver, Houston, Portland,
Oregon or Kansas City, Kansas? Tune in to
win great prizes with **Northern Light's Indy
500 Radio promotion!** Click here for details.

Special Editions™

In-depth coverage of major news stories,
edited and compiled by our team of librarians
and updated weekly.

Campaign 2000   European Economic Union
Electronic Commerce   Indy 500
Disability Insurance   More Special Editions™...

America's premier
oval-track, open-wheel
series has the new
name "Indy Racing Northern Light Series™"
as well as a new logo. More ...

User Information

Accolades   Link to Northern Light
Advertising   Press releases
Contact Northern Light   Privacy policy
Download title list   Register URL
Family-friendly resources   Search techniques
Forgot password   Set up a Member Account
IE4 or IE5 Users   Update account info
Jobs at Northern Light   usgovsearch.com

www.webcrawler.com

 ◎ visit the AT&T Communication Center

Search and Channels

[   ] Search

auctions   yellow pages   maps   product finder   chat now!
people finder   horoscopes   classifieds   stock quotes
weather   email lookup   city guides   more

Free Unlimited 56K Web Access

Autos
new, used, classifieds...

Careers
write a resume, find a job...

Computers & Internet
software, hardware...

Education
colleges, k-12...

Entertainment
TV, movies, music...

Games
online games, downloads...

Health
diet tips, medical info...

Home & Real Estate
buy, rent, finance...

Kids & Family
CTW family workshop...

Money & Investing
track stocks, invest...

My Page
personalize your page...

News - New!
today's top headlines...

People & Chat - New!
make friends, get advice...

Relationships
advice, personals...

Shopping
deals, product finder...

Small Business
taxes, legal issues...

Sports & Recreation
scores, highlights...

Travel
fares, reservations...

Inside WebCrawler

Play Online Games Now
Games: Demos and Downloads
Find Your Dream Job

Headline News

Updated: Saturday, May 27 8:14 PM ET

- o Canadian Town Buries Five E.Coli Victims
- o Long Time Foes Prepare to Rule Northern Ireland
- o Gore Touts U.S. Missile Defense Plan Ahead of Summit

Webcrawler Toolbox

Each day we bring you simple tools to save you time and money.

- o Free 56K Web Access
- o Daily Trivia Quiz
- o Online Address Book
- o Share Photos Online

See our complete list of tools.

A Word From Our Sponsors...

1-800-FlOWERS.COM
Make a Grad Glad!

Global Excite: Australia · France · Germany · Japan · Netherlands · Sweden · U.K.
WebCrawler Direct · Bookmark WebCrawler · Advertise on WebCrawler
· Add your URL

home || my page || email || help || about Excite

Microsoft Internet Explorer

Privacy Statement | Y2K Statement(s)

www.yahoo.com

What's New   Check Email   Personalize   Help

Yahoo! Auctions   The more people who enter *webshop*   **Win $10K from**
DSS, Britney Spears, tickets   the more prizes we give away Click here   NetZero ISP

[Search field]   **Search** advanced search

Shopping - **Auctions** - Yellow Pages - People Search - Maps - Travel - Classifieds - Personals - Games - Chat - **Clubs**
Mail - Calendar - Messenger - **Companion** - My Yahoo! - News - Sports - Weather - TV - Stock Quotes - more...

Yahoo! Shopping - Thousands of stores. Millions of products.

Departments	Stores	Features
· Apparel	· Gap	· J. K. Rowling
· Luxury	· 1-800-Flowers	· Gift Ideas
· Computers	· Banana Republic	· Special Offers
· Electronics	· Macy's	· Digital Cameras
· Flowers		
· Sports		
· Music		
· Video/DVD		

In the News
- Ulster Unionists back power-sharing
- Clinton releases new US diet guidelines
- 'Killer Resume' e-mail virus spreads
- Playoffs - NBA, NHL

  more...

Arts & Humanities
Literature, Photography...

News & Media
Full Coverage, Newspapers, TV...

Marketplace
- Y! Travel - buy tickets, check arrival times
- Free 56K ISP and email
- Looking for a car? job? house? date?

  more...

Business & Economy
B2B, Shopping, Finance, Jobs...

Recreation & Sports
Sports, Travel, Autos, Outdoors...

Computers & Internet
Internet, WWW, Software, Games...

Reference
Libraries, Dictionaries, Quotations...

Inside Yahoo!
- Y! Movies - M:I-2, Dinosaur, Gladiator
- Planning a party? Send an invite
- Yahoo! Photos - upload, share, and print pictures
- Y! Mobile - Yahoo! on your phone

  more...

Education
College and University, K-12...

Regional
Countries, Regions, US States...

Entertainment
Cool Links, Movies, Humor, Music...

Science
Animals, Astronomy, Engineering...

Government
Elections, Military, Law, Taxes...

Social Science
Archaeology, Economics, Languages...

Health
Medicine, Diseases, Drugs, Fitness...

Society & Culture
People, Environment, Religion...

World Yahoo!s *Europe* : Denmark - France - Germany - Italy - Norway - Spain - Sweden - UK & Ireland
Pacific Rim : Asia - Australia & NZ - **China** - Chinese - HK - Japan - Korea - Singapore - Taiwan
Americas : **Argentina** - Brazil - Canada - Mexico - Spanish

Yahoo! Get Local LA - NYC - SF Bay - Chicago - more...   [ ] **Enter Zip Code**

Other Autos - Careers - Digital - Entertainment - **Event Guide** - Greetings - Health - **Invites** - Net Events
Message Boards - Movies - Music - Real Estate - Small Business - Y! Internet Life - Yahooligans!

Yahoo! prefers **VISA**

How to Suggest a Site - Company Info - Copyright Policy - Terms of Service - Contributors - Openings at Yahoo!

A Buffalo Pottery Deldare Humidor purchased for $237.00 at www.cyrbid.com.

Three pieces of pressed glass in the pattern called "New Hampshire" or "Bent Buckle."

CHAPTER 2
COMPUTER BUYING 101

If you haven't bought a computer yet, you're probably totally confused by the choices. The most basic decision is *PC* (a generic term for personal computer of the IBM or IBM-clone variety) or *Macintosh*, and it gets harder from there. If you already have a computer feel free to skip this chapter unless you're considering upgrading; if not read on and gain useful information that will help you make your decision.

First, I'm not about to get in the middle of the PC versus Macintosh debate—it can get too emotional. People who have used Macs from the beginning swear by them, saying they're more dependable and easier to use. They frequently bristle at the mention of PC users claiming these same traits about their computers. What I will say is this—the vast majority of the business community has turned to the PC. Because of that, most software developers create their programs for the PC, making it much easier to find what you need if you're on a PC platform. The one exception is the graphics arts industry, where the Mac is still viewed as the platform of choice and having a Mac means being more compatible with the rest of the industry. This is also changing, and in fact this book was produced totally on a PC. Unless you intend to use your computer to do desktop publishing in your spare time, choosing a PC will give you many more choices for business applications, schoolwork, and games—the things that many of us like to do when not visiting the online auctions. The introduction of the *iMac* was aimed specifically at putting a dent in the markets where Macintosh now lags, and the Macintosh *G4* was touted as the fastest desktop computer available when the calendar rolled over to the year 2000. Macintosh is definitely alive and well, but for now the PC gives you more choices.

When considering how much power to buy, you need to evaluate how your computer will be used. On the PC platform in particular, processor speeds seem to double from one year to the next so you can be assured that what you buy today will be yesterday's news within six months. What you need to understand about this annoying rule of computer obsolescence is that it doesn't matter how quickly your machine is left behind as long as it does the things you need it to do. In fact, if you're going to use your computer primarily for Internet access and word processing, you definitely don't need the latest and greatest.

A PC processor with a speed of 400 *megahertz* (Mhz), considered state of the art in 1999, is generally viewed as average-to-slow in 2000. Because of being "obsolete," it can be bought for well under $1,000 and will supply all of the raw power you need for basic computing needs. If you plan to work with large image files in a graphic arts environment or play the latest computer games you will want to invest in a faster processor, but for the small files you'll use to post photos on the Internet 400Mhz is plenty.

Your next decision will probably revolve around a choice between a *Pentium* processor versus a *Celeron* processor, both made by *Intel,* or possibly a processor made by competitor *AMD*. Both the Celeron and AMD chipsets got some bad press when they were first introduced, some deservedly so. They have since improved dramatically. If you are purchasing a new computer primarily for Internet access and small office duties, do not hesitate to buy one with either one of these processors. If you want to stick with Intel, the Celeron is a formidable alternative to the more expensive Pentium processors.

To give you an idea of what you can purchase for around $1,000.00, I recently got a phone call from my daughter who is a graduate student majoring in psychology and has a definite need for some computer power. She was still using an older 120Mhz computer with a 14,400K modem and wanted me to recommend a new system. I offered to do the shopping for her, and came up with the following deal for almost exactly $1,000. Don't worry if you don't understand all of the jargon used here—I'll explain more later.

Dell Dimension 400Mhz Celeron processor with 128K cache and 4MB Graphics
Logitech First Mouse+
Dell Quiet Key keyboard
Dell 800F 15" color monitor
32MB SDRAM (we upgraded to 64MB for $59.00 extra)
4.3GB hard drive
1.44MB floppy drive
Soundblaster 64V PCI sound card
Harman/Kardon HK-195 speakers
6X variable DVD-ROM drive

26

US Robotics V.90 56K telephony WinModem
Epson Stylus 660 color printer
Windows 98
McAfee Virusscan virus software
Microsoft Works Suite99
1 Year DellNet Internet access service

That's right! A 400Mhz computer complete with a color monitor, color printer, 56K modem, a DVD-ROM which also plays CD-ROMs, virus software, office software, a one year warranty and a free year of Internet access for around $1,000.00! This offering was found on the Internet by buying direct from Dell at *http://www.dell.com*, proving that good deals are out there.

If you want to hear the sounds (music files, radio, etc.) that the Internet can make, and you will, buy a system with a soundcard and speakers. You should definitely invest in a 56K modem (see Chapter 3—Choosing an Internet Service Provider for more on modems). If you buy a multimedia (MMX) system it should already have the soundcard and speakers bundled right in, but I don't recommend buying MMX technology unless you are purchasing a used machine and are a graphic artist or gaming fanatic. Today's processor speeds make MMX an obsolete technology.

RAM (random access memory) is second in importance to your processor speed when it comes to system performance—the more RAM you get with your computer the better. 32MB is considered standard today, so start there and as you progress you may want to add on. Adding memory is one of the least expensive upgrades you can make, so it won't be costly if you decide later you want more.

The SDRAM mentioned in the computer my daughter purchased is *synchronous dynamic random access memory,* which is faster than previous generations of random access memory. It sends data from the main memory to the system processor more efficiently, and is a must for computers that utilize the new 100Mhz bus speeds. You should make sure you are getting SDRAM with any new computer purchase.

Your hard drive is where everything you need to operate your computer is stored. Hard drives are rated in terms of the amount of data they can hold. Just a few years ago the largest hard drives were rated in megabytes (MB), but today are measured in gigabytes (GB). To help you comprehend the amount of data we're talking about here, know that a single character is the equivalent of one byte. From there measurements are as follows…

1024 Bytes = 1 Kilobyte
1024 Kilobytes = 1 Megabyte
1024 Megabytes = 1 Gigabyte
1024 Gigabytes = 1 Terabyte

Most software today is loaded onto your computer from a *CD-ROM*. The faster the drive the more quickly large applications should be loaded. However, some software manufacturers prepare their data in a format that only allows your CD-ROM to read them at slower speeds, so having the fastest drive isn't critical.

Games are played from CD-ROMs, and the same music CDs you listen to in your car or home CD player will play in your computer CD-ROM drive (provided of course you have the proper software, a sound-card, and speakers). A 32X drive has become fairly common, but don't fret if the computer you like best has a slower drive. Unless you are a gaming fanatic you probably won't notice much difference.

The next evolution of the CD-ROM is already here in the form of the *DVD-ROM*. DVD-ROM brings enhanced multimedia capabilities to your system, including the ability to watch movies on it. DVD-ROM is backward compatible with CD-ROM, so your software installation CD's will still work and you can still play your audio CD's. At the present time movies on DVD-ROM are just beginning to surface, but they will be as prolific as VHS in the future.

Unless you buy a package like the one outlined earlier in this chapter you will have to purchase a monitor separately from your computer. Special offers will sometimes bundle them together, but in today's market more often than not when you purchase a computer you don't get the monitor with it. A 14-inch monitor may have you squinting occasionally and a 17-inch monitor is an unnecessary expense unless you routinely work with page layout spreads or spreadsheets. A 15-inch monitor is fine for general use, but as prices come down a 17-inch monitor, once considered a luxury, will become much more common on home systems.

Be aware that the *resolution* of the monitor affects the size and clarity of your display. Anything less than a resolution of 640x480 is unacceptable today. You can change the resolution of your monitor through the Control Panel of your computer. On a Windows 95 or 98 computer click **Start-Settings-Control Panel**. In the window that opens double-click **Display**. The resulting window will have a tab you can click for **Settings**. You will now see a slide bar that controls the resolution of your monitor and can experiment with different settings until you get the one you're most comfortable with.

Also check the *refresh rate* of the video card driving the monitor. The refresh rate is the speed with which it redraws and image on the screen. Video cards are rated in Hz (hertz), which is the amount of electrical pulses emitted per second. Don't settle for anything less than a 60Hz refresh rate.

The 1.44MB floppy disk has been a standard for years, and unless you come across a real relic at a yard sale every PC you find will have one. The name "floppy" was derived from the earliest days of computing, when the first home computers used a removable disk measuring 5.25" in diameter that really was flexible, and would "flop" around when you held it by one corner. New Macintosh computers no longer ship with a floppy drive; if you want one you must buy it separately. Unless you have special "decoding" software a PC cannot read a Mac disk and vice versa.

Macintosh gambled with the introduction of the *iMac* and, more recently, the *G4,* and did not equip them with floppy disk drives. The reasoning was that the floppy would soon be obsolete, the future of computing was the Internet and larger storage capacity, and to hold down costs to be more competitive. I believe this to be sound reasoning, but Macintosh may have been a bit ahead of their time. The average computer user still needs a floppy drive, and until the benefits of the larger capacity removable storage drives are recognized by the overall business community floppies still reign supreme.

If you are in the graphic arts business and routinely move large graphic files from place to place, you should opt for either a built-in Iomega ZIP or JAZ drive, or a CDRW drive that allows you to burn your own CDs. The ZIP comes in either a 100MB or 250MB size, utilizing a removable cartridge that is not much bigger than a floppy. The JAZ cartridge is a bit bigger yet but can hold either 1GB or 2GB of data. Currently CDs hold 650-800MB of data.

Here then is my recommendation for a basic PC that you intend to use primarily for word processing, Internet access, and general use. This is actually a generously powered machine, but in today's market there's not enough difference in price to buy any less. Talk to the vendor you purchase your computer from about your needs and ask them to recommend and explain additional features available. You can purchase a computer with these specifications for less than one thousand dollars, and if you look hard enough you will be able to include the monitor and a printer for that price.

400Mhz Processor
64MB RAM
3.2GB Hard Drive
1.44MB Floppy Drive
32X CD ROM Drive
15-Inch Color Monitor (640x480 resolution minimum)
4MB video card w/60Hz Refresh Rate
56K Modem
Soundcard
Speakers

If you already have a computer with Internet access and are considering upgrading, you might want to get your feet wet with online auctions by bidding on computers and/or computer parts. Most of the major online auctions have a computer category, and mail order companies like PC Mall hold online auctions at their sites too.

A Nippon Raised Relief Humidor with green wreath mark. Internet bidding for this item reached $800.00.

A milk glass hen candy dish with a blue colored head and glass eyes.

Below:
A "Blue Ware" jardinière by Weller decorated with four caryatids, made before 1920.

A tin mold to make candy chinamen.

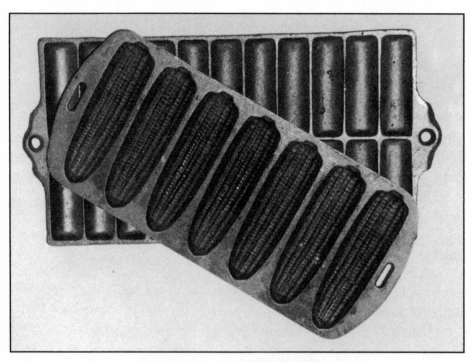

Two cast iron cornbread molds.

CHAPTER 3
CHOOSING AN INTERNET SERVICE PROVIDER

You have a computer with a modem, now what? How do you find an Internet Service Provider (*ISP*)? How do you sift through the seemingly endless technology offerings of the different providers? You don't have to understand the difference between a SLIP/PPP and UUCP connection, but you should be able to recognize a good deal from an average one.

The Free Way

You no longer need to pay a monthly fee for Internet access, although you give up certain conveniences in doing so. If you are on a tight budget, don't mind having advertisements taking up a six-inch band of your monitor space, and can live with a limited-feature e-mail address, free access might be OK for you.

Several sites offer free access, but you have to already be online to get to them, right? Not necessarily. Ask a friend with Internet access to download one or two of the free Internet programs outlined below for you (most of them fit on a floppy disk) and you can then install it on your computer. You'll need a modem and phone line but that's it—the Internet access will be free. You can also use one of the promotional CDs that come in the mail for free hours with one of the national providers like *America Online*—if you don't have any ask around and you'll probably find someone who does. Use the promo hours online to download the free service and try it out. If you like it, cancel the paid service before the free hours are expired. One recommendation I would make is to download at least two of the free services—that way if one routinely gives you busy signals, slow connections, outages, or ceases to exist you'll have a backup to keep you going.

Most of the major search engines combine useful Internet search tools with free services. AltaVista *(http://www.altavista.com)* offers free Internet access and a free e-mail address to go with it. Yahoo! and Kmart have teamed up to bring you free Internet access through Bluelight.com *(http://www.bluelight.com)* where you combine free access with a Yahoo! free e-mail address. Lycos *(http://www.lycos.com),* Excite *(http://www.excite.com)* and many others have all added free access to their list of services. Make sure whatever service(s) you sign up for provides a local access number for your modem to dial—if you have to dial long distance to get online the service isn't free anymore, is it?

When Free Doesn't Cut It...

Start by asking your friends and business associates who they use. They should be able to provide phone numbers for you to begin your quest and possibly even promotional disks from an ISP with some free hours to try their service. The national ISPs, particularly *America Online* and *Earthlink*, distribute a large number of these trial disks.

The newspapers, especially in larger metropolitan areas, will likely have ads for local providers you can contact. As you read on you will find information to help you evaluate whether you want to try a national or local provider.

Don't overlook the major phone companies—AT&T, Sprint, MCI, Bell Atlantic, and many others all provide Internet access. If you're in the market for a local provider try the phone book under categories like Computers-Communications or Internet Service Providers.

Here are some questions to ask an Internet Service Provider you are considering.

√ Do You Have A Local Access Number?

Avoid dialing long distance to connect to your ISP, unless you live in a remote area and have no choice. When your ISP is a long distance call away, you pay not only their monthly access charge but also long distance charges to your phone company for the ENTIRE time you are connected. The national carriers provide local numbers for large metropolitan areas, but there are still regions where they are not available. If this happens to you, investigate whether or not you have a regional/local company offering Internet access. If you do, consider signing up with them as long as they satisfy the requirements outlined in this chapter.

If one of the national providers offers things you really want (some people can't live without their *America Online* chat rooms) you might be able to make a special arrangement with a local ISP to use their service as a way to get connected to the national provider. You'll be paying a monthly fee to both, but it still might be lower than paying long distance charges for access. Make sure you let the national provider know you are paying double to get their service because they have no local access number and ask for a reduced rate.

√ Do You Use SLIP/PPP?

Here's one of those technical terms we're trying to avoid, but this is one you should ask. With SLIP/PPP, you have direct access to the Internet through your ISPs server. Some ISPs route you through a series of computers and servers before you actually connect. There are many reasons why you should connect directly, the most obvious being speed and less chance of downtime. The more computers you pass through on your way to the Internet the better chance you have of one of them breaking your connection. Suffice to say you want the direct access provided by SLIP/PPP—don't settle for less. And for those of you who just *have* to know, SLIP is an acronym for Serial Line Internet Protocol and PPP is Point-to-Point Protocol. There, feel better?

√ What Types of Accounts Do You Offer?

Most ISPs will offer at least a monthly rate for unlimited service and an hourly, or metered rate. Some offer discounts to senior citizens and students—be sure to ask.

√ What Is Your Ratio of Subscribers to Modems?

The more modems your ISP has the better. A good ratio if you have unlimited access is 9:1 (nine users to one modem) and for metered access 14:1. Higher numbers don't necessarily spell trouble, but unusually high ratios can mean busy signals when you dial in and slower connection speeds.

√ What Is the Cost For Each Type of Account?

Monthly charges vary more than you might think. I've seen monthly rates for unlimited access as low as $9.95 for a local ISP in a rural area to $26.95 for the bigger national providers. Make sure you inquire about installation fees—some charge them even though the "installation" is done from their office. In the beginning you might consider opting for the higher cost provider if they offer top-notch tech support to help you through the learning curve. Once you're a savvy user consider switching to the low-cost provider if they meet your basic requirements.

√ Do You Charge For Disk Space On Your Server?

When you start taking photos with that new digital camera you couldn't live without you'll need space on your ISP's server to post them for the world to see. If you're in the market for an unlimited access account look for a provider that offers some server space as a part of your monthly fee. Many offer 2 megabytes at no additional charge, and this is adequate for the average user.

√ Will My Modem Talk to Your Modem?

Modems are like "walkie-talkies" for computers. If your computer has one, and it is connected to a phone line, you can "talk" to someone else who has another modem. Unlike walkie-talkies, modems simply transfer information bits; you don't actually speak. But modems are the lifeblood of sending and receiving information on the Internet and using e-mail.

Modems come in both *external* (sits on your desk) and *internal* (resides inside your computer) varieties, and computer people used to argue endlessly about which was best. They're priced about the same, and the fact is they both perform about the same, so it comes down to whether or not you like to watch flashing lights when you're sending data. I recommend going with an internal modem, even though it may cost a few dollars more to have a professional install it in your computer. The less clutter on your desk the better!

Most modems will connect to each other, but with newer technologies being invented all the time you should ask the question. Hopefully you know your modem speed and manufacturer—if not, check the *Control Panel* of a computer running Windows. You will see a modem icon: double click it and you will get some general information about your modem, which may help the ISP you are talking to determine if you are compatible with their system. If you don't know what type of modem you have and can't find out, ask if there is a test you can perform that will assure you can connect with them. At the very worst you may have to buy a new, higher speed modem, which isn't a bad idea anyway if you're using one several years old. Less than $100 will get you a top-notch model, but you may go a bit over $100 if someone else installs it for you.

Modem speeds are measured in kilo-bits per second (Kbps) along with a number rating. If you have a modem with a top speed of 14,400 or 28,800 consider upgrading to at least 33,600 and preferably 56,000 (56K in computer lingo). These higher speed modems have dropped considerably in price since first being introduced. If you opt for a 56K modem be sure you get one that uses the recently adopted V.90 standard; all ISPs are required to support modems with this technology.

√ How Many Mail Accounts Do I Get?

This may be explained to you when you ask about the types of accounts, but if it isn't make sure you're getting at least one e-mail address. Without one you can't send or receive electronic mail, unless you subscribe to one of the free Internet-hosted services. These accounts, offered on the home page of several major search engines, are often slow and cumbersome to use. You will quickly find that your own ISP-provided e-mail account is one of the most useful reasons for having Internet access.

√ Do You Offer All Available Newsgroups?

Newsgroups are informative and entertaining, and as you become more experienced you'll find yourself subscribing to a few. You can interact with an international audience about almost anything you can imagine, including your favorite collectibles.

Individual newsgroups are formed to discuss one primary topic. The term *Usenet* refers to the entire newsgroup community collectively. Newsgroup names begin with a prefix that denotes a general guide to their category. These categories are expanding constantly, but some of the types of groups you will encounter are...

alt	Discussion of alternative/informal subjects
comp	Discussion of computer science and related topics
news	Discussion of Usenet itself
rec	Discussion of recreational activities
sci	Discussion of scientific research
talk	Debate on controversial issues
misc	Groups that don't fall into established categories

Specific newsgroups exist for dolls (**rec.collecting.dolls**), teddy bears (**alt.collecting.teddy-bears**), and many other collectibles. Some newsgroups contain primarily items for sale, but some share information, and the things you can learn by participating in one or two good ones about your favorite collectible is amazing. Some of the groups are very active, with hundreds of messages being posted daily. Others have less traffic; feel free to monitor several until you find one that seems comfortable. You should be able to access newsgroups from your e-mail program, as well as search for newsgroups containing a certain word or words you specify (i.e. antiques).

Be aware that certain newsgroups have controversial subjects as their content, and some ISPs censor these. If you're planning to join a newsgroup with content you think may be at risk, inquire as to whether all newsgroups are supported.

Once you've signed on, always remember when communicating with groups to choose your words carefully—more than one novice newsgroup user has been *flamed* by the group for a poor choice of vocabulary or topic. Flaming is the online equivalent of the lecture you got from your mother when you were bad, but is often a lot nastier than good old Mom would have been. Seeing it in print can have a more negative impact than the spoken word, and the fact that you're being flamed by virtual strangers makes it very uncomfortable. It's a good idea to just read the posts from a newsgroup that interests you for a week or two before jumping in. This way you can get a feel for the types of people you'll be interacting with.

√ How Does Your Tech Support Work?

Is it staffed 24 hours? If not, what hours may I call and what is the number? If the call is not local, do you have a toll free number? Do you have a Web site and/or online support? Will you help me configure my computer to communicate with your equipment? Is there any software I have to buy in order to communicate with your equipment?

Once you have the answers to all of these questions, call the tech support number to see if you get a live person, a recording, or get put on indefinite hold. Anything other than a live person answering relatively quickly should go in the minus column when considering this ISP.

Once you choose your ISP you have one more decision to make—whether or not you want to invest in a second phone line for your Internet access. If you plan to do a lot of online business it's pretty much a necessity. Even a part-time business online takes more time than you are probably thinking. As outlined in my companion book to this one, *The ABCs of Making Money Online,* the biggest surprise for most dealers expanding their business to the Internet is the time investment it takes. That time online takes away from time your spouse and kids can spend talking on the phone, so consider a second line if for no other reason than to keep peace in the family.

Another thing you will want to consider is your phone bill and how to minimize costs. As stated earlier in this chapter, your first priority is to make sure the number you dial to connect is a local number. Next, find out if you are paying a flat rate for unlimited local calls. If you're not, you might want to switch to a flat rate depending on how often you plan to dial in to your ISP. If unlimited local calling is not available, inquire about *call packs,* which allow you to call the same phone number a specified amount of times for a flat fee.

You are now armed and ready to begin an adventure in learning the likes of which you've never seen. Be warned: the Internet is addictive!

Stamps, both foreign and domestic.

"The Famous Automobile Card Game," "Touring," by Parker Brothers.

Paper advertising pieces: a card for Ribbon Dental Cream by Colgate and a recipe book by the Enterprise Mfg. Co. of PA which was given away by Gimbel Brothers.

CHAPTER 4
FINDING ANTIQUES AND
COLLECTIBLES IN CYBERSPACE

There are many choices available online for buying and selling antiques and collectibles. The one used by more people than any other is eBay™, an online auction that routinely offers over four million items in so many different categories you can't possibly look at everything in the week it takes for a typical auction to expire. If you haven't already, read Chapter 5—Using eBay™ to get the details. Once you know your way around eBay™ you can feel secure in trying out some other online auctions. Most of them operate in similar ways, and as you become familiar with buying this way you will find it easy to navigate through any online auction site.

What will you find online in the antiques and collectibles fields?, It would be easier to list the things you won't find. Furniture, not widely available at the online auctions at one time due mainly to the costs associated with shipping, has become commonplace. Buyers are paying as much as $250.00 to have large pieces shipped to them after winning auctions. Many online malls and individual shops also offer furniture, including some very high quality pieces.

The top ten sought after collectibles online varies weekly, is sometimes driven by current events, and depends on whom you talk to. During the late summer of 1998 Mark McGwire and Sammy Sosa collectibles were in high demand as they both chased, and eventually broke, the major league baseball home run record set by Roger Maris in 1961. One site ranks *BARBIE*® and Morgan silver dollars in the top ten routinely, while another mentions painted furniture, Pokémon, and gives no mention to *BARBIE*®. But no matter what collectible interests you, there is a very good chance you will be able to find it at an online auction.

Literally thousands of sites exist on the Internet to buy or sell antiques and collectibles. It is becoming more and more difficult to categorize them as many are offering auctions, retail shops, online price guides and more all under one roof. You can and should use search engines to find antiques and collectible sites, but to help get you started following is a list of some to whet your appetite.

GENERAL AUCTIONS/ONLINE COMMUNITIES

The information about the following online auctions was researched during May/June 2000. Several auction sites that I reviewed for *The ABCs of Collecting Online 2* have now gone out of business, and nobody is even close to challenging eBay™ yet. Still, it is worthwhile to check out some of these sites to see what types of merchandise they offer and their fee structures—some charge no fees at all. Others seem to draw collectors with similar interests—for instance, if you go for sports collectibles one place you should keep an eye on is auctions.com.

http://auctions.amazon.com

In addition to art, antiques and collectibles, amazon.com now offers a selection of top quality merchandise through an affiliation with the well-known auction house Sothebys. After you check out the regular auction site, find out what else is cooking at *http://sothebys.amazon.com*.

http://www.auctionaddict.com

Auction Addict has an attractive site that has always featured no placement fees, and as of April 19, 2000 they also stopped charging sales commissions. You can list items on this auction absolutely free! As one of the many newcomers to the online auction world during 1998, listings at first were few when compared to some of the established auctions. However, Auction Addict has steadily grown and whereas their largest category in late 1998 was Collectibles with 324 listings, that category in September 1999 had increased to over 2200 entries and in May 2000 had grown again to 3923. Overall, there were 21 categories with almost 9000 open listings in September 1999, growing to 25 categories and 22,500 listings by May 2000.

http://www.auctionport.com

Auction Port continues to survive in the online auction world, typically hovering right around 2000 listings in a wide range of categories. After increasing listing volume nearly 40% during their first year of operation, Auction Port has leveled off in the past six months and seems now to be experiencing minimal growth. The site is well designed, easy to use, and features chat forums with some of the categories. There are no basic listing fees to sellers.

http://www.auctions.com

Launched October 12, 1999, this site is easy to use, loads into your browser quickly, has a good variety of categories to choose from, and offers free basic listings. A recent check (May 2000) showed 28,865 total items up for bid, a slight decrease from the 30,164 items found eight months ago during research for the 2nd edition of this book. As it has been since I've been monitoring this site, the Sports Collectibles category was the most prolific at 12,387 entries, making up 43% of the total listings.

http://www.boxlot.com

Following a late-1999 advertising campaign in the antique trade papers, boxLot increased their exposure to more than 2000 listings in antiques and more than 8000 in collectibles, earning them a mention as a site to investigate.

http://www.buffalobid.com

After hanging tough for nearly two years, Buffalo Bid seems to have finally run out of gas. With total inventory down to 19 listings in May 2000 when just six months ago over 2000 lots of postcards and coins were available, it appears that the buffalo may be nearly extinct.

http://www.ebay.com

After almost five years eBay™ is still the king of the hill, having withstood the charge (so far) of Amazon.com and Yahoo! auctions. Instead of losing business to these challengers, eBay™ has increased in volume, routinely offering over four million items for sale at the same time. A recent site redesign gave eBay™ a more modern look, and their huge volume means that it's unusual to *not* find what you're looking for. See Chapter 5—Using eBay™ for step-by-step instructions on how to register and get going.

http://auctions.amazon.com

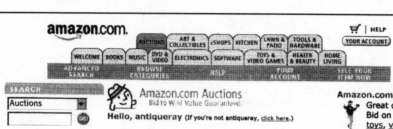

SEARCH

Auctions

BROWSE
- Arts & Antiques
- Books
- Coins & Stamps
- Collectibles
- Comics, Cards & Sci-Fi
- Computers & Software
- Electronics & Photography
- Jewelry, Gems & Watches
- Movies & Video
- Music
- Sports
- Toys & Games

➤ See all categories

sothebys.amazon.com
- NASCAR memorabilia
- Rare rock memorabilia
- Important stamps
- More Special Sales

LiveBid Auctions
- Unique consumer goods
- Industrial offerings
➤ More live auctions

✉ Sign up for e-mail recommendations.

Amazon.com Auctions
Bid to Win! Value Guaranteed.

Hello, antiqueray (If you're not antiqueray, click here.)

Boot up computer deals in our Computer SuperAuctions.

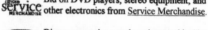

Attention, movie lovers: don't miss out on authentic Hollywood props or exclusive gear from *Gladiator*. Music maniacs can also bid on groovy concert posters from the 1960s and beyond.
See all Featured Sales

Fantastic Finds from Trusted Brands
We've teamed up with great partners to offer brand-new, high-quality products with low starting bids.

service MERCHANDISE Bid on DVD players, stereo equipment, and other electronics from Service Merchandise.

gear.com Discover sporting goods and apparel by North Face, Timberland, and others from Gear.com.

Items Featured Today
- Hand made Cigar box of 25 (premium brands)
- Secretly Record their CHAT conversations and EMAILS with Spector !
- EXCLUSIVE ITALIAN DINNER SET FOR 12!! A REAL DAYDREAM!!
- 1991 Bowman Chipper Jones & Ivan Rodriguez Both Gem Mint ASA 9.5 = PSA 10 = BGS
- Hemingway "FOR WHOM THE BELL TOLLS" FIRST PRINT W/DJ
- Ernest Hemingway "WINNER TAKES NOTHING" LEATHER MINT!!!!
➤ See all Featured Items

Summer Memories
From evenings at the ballpark to lazy

Amazon.com Outlet
Great deals! Bid on new toys, video games, electronics, and dot-com wear sold by Amazon.com Outlet.

Dollar Deals
Star Trek, VHS Pikachu, and more auctions starting at just a dollar.

Favorite Discoveries
1. Computer SuperAuctions
2. Divine vinyl
3. Led Zeppelin CDs
4. 1966 Emmy Award
5. *Wolverine* and more comics

Going, Going, Gone!
What is this?

- Puyo Pop (NEOGEO) - Amazon.com Outlet - - Time Left: 00:04:16
- 2 inch (50mm) Snowflake Obsidian Sphere -- Time Left: 00:05:09
- Pokemon Action FLIPZ Lenticular Collecti -- Time Left:

http://www.auctionport.com

Your Online Auctions for Antique, Collectibles & More When Shopping Online Auctions!

AuctionPort *The Best Antiques, Collectibles and More That Auctions Have To Offer*

Home Listings Register Buyers Sellers Live Rooms Featured MyPort Search Help Guide

Saturday May 27 2000

Categories

Antiques & Art
Big Ticket Items
Books & Magazines
Coins & Currency
Collectibles
Computers
Consumer
Dolls & Figures
Glass
Jewelry & Timepieces
Miscellaneous
Music & Movies
Pottery & Porcelain
Sports & Trading
Cards
Stamps
Toys
all categories...

[Search] options

Check out what's new at Auction Port!

Personal Online Auctions and the Auction Port Gallery
"An Antique and Collectibles Experience"

Welcome to Auction Port Online Auctions, see how to get started with our easy and fun auction community. FREE seller services like image hosting, hit counters and no insertion or standard listing fee! Auction Port registration is not required to browse the community >>> any questions....?

Highlights	**Resources**	**Theme Months**
Auction Rooms	**Personal Shopper**	CURRENT THEME:
Auctions Ending	**Appraisal Wizard**	5/1 - **Jewelry Classics**
New Auctions	**Live Chat Forums**	
Hot Auctions	**Free Classifieds**	UPCOMING THEMES:
Hot Categories	**Wish List Board**	6/1 - **Book Classics**
Live Auctions	**Bookstore**	7/1 - **Glass Classics**
Just Listed	**Internet Resources**	
more features....	*more resources....*	*check the Theme Calendar...*

See These Featured Auctions....

Photo = **See Enlarged Photo**   Description = **Go to Item**   = **Reserve Auction**

REPLICA BYZANTINE EARRINGS in Silver	Seen: 16	Current: $9.00	Ends: 6/21 2:14 PM ET
RAM KUMAR (b.1924), "HA" 60's Beautiful Abstract	Seen: 16	Current: $2500.00	Ends: 6/1 8:28 AM ET
MOSAIC FLOWER BROOCH (1950)	Seen: 9	Current: $16.00	Ends: 6/4 2:37 PM ET
AGATE and MARCASITE MASONIC RING in S. S.	Seen: 6	Current: $23.95	Ends: 6/9 2:27 PM ET
MARCASITE BROOCH in STERLING SILVER (Reproduction)	Seen: 4	Current: $23.95	Ends: 6/9 2:27 PM ET

>>> **see more featured....**

[Listings] [Sell Item] [Register] [Users Services] [Featured] [New] [Ending] [Bookstore] [Help] [Site Map]

http://www.auctions.com

  [ ] SEARCH

Advanced Search   View All Categories   My auctions.com   Merchant Central   Showcase Auctions!

Getting Started: How to Sell and Bid | Register Free | List an Item | Shop | Site Help | Contact Us

Categories

:Antiques & Decorative Arts
:Autos, Boats, Planes & more
:Beanies and More Beans
:Books, Autographs & Paper
:Business Goods & Services
:Collectibles & Memorabilia
:Comics, Cards, Figures, SciFi
:Computers
:Dolls, Toys & Models
:Electronics
:Grab Bag
:Home, Garden & Pet Supplies
:Jewelry & Fashion
:Music, TV & Entertainment
:Sporting Goods & Recreation
:Sports Cards & Collectibles
:Stamps, Coins & Currency
 see all categories >>

 The OFFICIAL auction service of NHL.com

 Official Auction Service Provider to Elton John

our partner sites:

Auctions in Australia
Auctions in the United Kingdom
Auctions in Canada
apartments.com
cars.com
HomeHunter sites
MovingCenter
NewHomeNetwork.com

 PayPal.com CLICK HERE

Ringo Starr!!!

Ringo Starr and CENTURY 21® team up to bring you some one-of-a-kind collectibles that you won't find anywhere else!

Jewel Auction!

Her rare recordings and personal items are on the block! Every winning bid benefits charity.

Golf anyone?

Bid on **TWO** All-Tournament Grounds Passes to the 100th US Open Golf Championship at Pebble Beach! Proceeds to benefit the Special Olympics.

Merchants

Hockey Coins
Limited Edition 24K
Gold Plate!

: **Sparkling Spring Specials!**
Lavish Jewelry with a starting bid of just $1.00!

TekLinc.com
Deep discount liquidators of quality merchandise.

Merchants Online
Shop with our top merchants.
Bargains abound!

Merchant Central
Your own auction page or site!

Virtual Mall
An out-of-store experience.

 TRUST'e site privacy statement

auctions.com - The Real Deal

http://www.boxlot.com

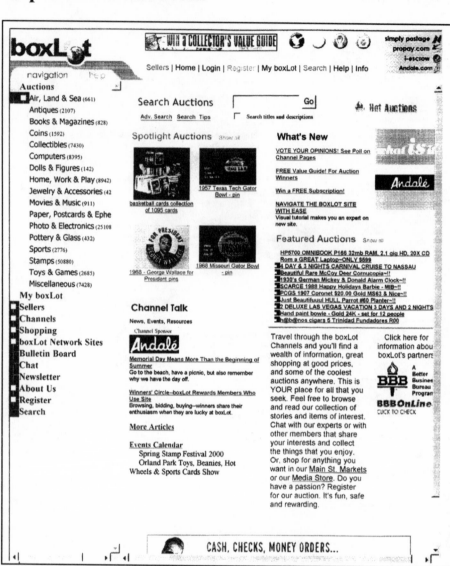

Sellers | Home | Login | Register | My boxLot | Search | Help | Info

navigation   help

Auctions

- Air, Land & Sea (661)
- Antiques (2107)
- Books & Magazines (828)
- Coins (1592)
- Collectibles (7430)
- Computers (8395)
- Dolls & Figures (142)
- Home, Work & Play (8942)
- Jewelry & Accessories (42)
- Movies & Music (911)
- Paper, Postcards & Ephe
- Photo & Electronics (25108)
- Pottery & Glass (432)
- Sports (2776)
- Stamps (50880)
- Toys & Games (2685)
- Miscellaneous (7428)

My boxLot

- Sellers
- Channels
- Shopping
- boxLot Network Sites
- Bulletin Board
- Chat
- Newsletter
- About Us
- Register
- Search

Search Auctions

[ ] Go

Adv. Search   Search Tips   ☐ Search titles and descriptions

Hot Auctions

Spotlight Auctions Show all

basketball cards collection of 1095 cards

1957 Texas Tech Gator Bowl - pin

1968 - George Wallace for President pins

1968 Missouri Gator Bowl - pin

Channel Talk

News, Events, Resources

Channel Sponsor

Andalé

Memorial Day Means More Than the Beginning of Summer
Go to the beach, have a picnic, but also remember why we have the day off.

Winners' Circle--boxLot Rewards Members Who Use Site
Browsing, bidding, buying--winners share their enthusiasm when they are lucky at boxLot.

More Articles

Events Calendar
Spring Stamp Festival 2000
Orland Park Toys, Beanies, Hot Wheels & Sports Cards Show

What's New

VOTE YOUR OPINIONS! See Poll on Channel Pages

FREE Value Guide! For Auction Winners

Win a FREE Subscription!

NAVIGATE THE BOXLOT SITE WITH EASE
Visual tutorial makes you an expert on new site.

Featured Auctions Show all

HP5700 OMNIBOOK P166 32mb RAM, 2.1 gig HD, 20X CD Rom a GREAT Laptop--ONLY $599
4 DAY & 3 NIGHTS CARNIVAL CRUISE TO NASSAU
Beautiful Rare McCoy Deer Cornucopia~!!
1930's German Mickey & Donald Alarm Clock~!!
SCARCE 1988 Happy Holidays Barbie - MIB~!!
PCGS 1907 Coronet $20.00 Gold MS63 & Nice~!!
Just Beautifuuul HULL Parrot #60 Planter~!!
2 DELUXE LAS VEGAS VACATION 3 DAYS AND 2 NIGHTS
Hand paint bowie - Gold 24K - set for 12 people
h@b@nos cigars 5 Trinidad Fundadores R00

Travel through the boxLot Channels and you'll find a wealth of information, great shopping at good prices, and some of the coolest auctions anywhere. This is YOUR place for all that you seek. Feel free to browse and read our collection of stories and items of interest. Chat with our experts or with other members that share your interests and collect the things that you enjoy. Or, shop for anything you want in our Main St. Markets or our Media Store. Do you have a passion? Register for our auction. It's fun, safe and rewarding.

Click here for information abou boxLot's partners

BBB
A Better Business Program

BBBOnLine
CLICK TO CHECK

http://www.buffalobid.com

http://www.ebay.com

home | my eBay | site map | sign in

Browse | Sell | Services | Search | Help | Community

the world's online marketplace

welcome new users

register

new to eBay? | how do I bid? | how do I sell?

why eBay is safe

what are you looking for?

 Smart Search

Specialty Sites

Automotive
Business Exchange
Great Collections

Categories

Antiques & Art
Books, Movies & Music
Coins & Stamps
Collectibles
Computers
Dolls, Figures
Jewelry, Gemstones
Photo & Electronics
Pottery & Glass
Sports
Toys, Bean Bag Plush
Everything Else
all categories...

Over 4 million items for sale!

Global Sites

eBay Australia
eBay Canada
eBay Germany
eBay Japan
eBay United Kingdom

Hot Picks

Great Grabs for Graduates - Gift Giving Guide

Local Trading

Appliances   Furniture
Electronics   Real Estate
Sporting Goods *more...*

Pick a region ▼

Go!

Browse by Themes

Chinatown page
Fashion page
Comics page

Animation ▼

Go!

Featured Items

all gallery items...

Cc Cowboys: Blodscbrodre * Rare / Mint
@@ Wholesale Set Of 4 Stock Pots @@
2000 Sacagawea DENVER MINT $$ coins*r*us
Disappearing dime magic trick - Unbelievable!
Drop 88 pounds for Summer, NEW FAT BURNER!
Professional Gourmet Cutlery Set with Case
all featured items...

Don't Miss...

Rosie

Charity

Bid for a good cause!

Get items **FAST!** Buy with Billpoint!

Spotlight's On...

New eBay Motors site!

eBay Power Trading

E*TRADE

eBay's advertising partnership

http://www.cyrbid.com

Just eight short months ago I touted Cyrbid auction as one to watch in *The ABCs of Collecting Online 2.* What happened? By May 2000 they dropped to an inventory of just four listings. I was so impressed with this site in the early going that I decided to contact the management to see what had happened, but requests to interview Jim Cyr of New England's Cyr Auction have gone unanswered. This really did look like a good one at the outset, with quality items going for reasonable prices. Hopefully Cyrbid is experiencing a stumble and not a permanent fall.

http://www.ehammer.com

This site was launched a few years ago with a lot of advertising and, being backed by *Maine Antique Digest*, I expected it by this time to be a leader in the online auction community. Instead I have been surprised to find both the quantity and quality of listings drop over the past nine months, with around 2150 items available in May 2000. The category with the most listings was jewelry.

http://auctions.excite.com

Keeping up with competition the likes of amazon.com and Yahoo! is tough, but Excite auctions represent themselves well. Excite gives you some options that almost make their site a cross between a storefront and auction, like being able to list an item for a month.

http://www.haggle.com

Primarily computers and electronics—if you deal in these items or are looking for a new computer system this is one to check out, with thousands of computers and parts up for bid.

http://www.kaleden.com

Kaleden.com is a marketplace for the antique collector, with auctions, dealer directories, online malls, a price guide, and other value-added resources for collectors.

http://www.manions.com

Resembling a traditional auction more than an Internet one, Manion's will handle your items for you on a consignment basis. First, you send them a list of items you would like to consign (minimum value $20.00) with a description and your preferred reserve price, and wait to hear if your items are approved for auction. You then pack up your items and ship them with a list of what is in each box to Manions. Lots with values of $50.00 or more will be photographed, with pictures appearing in an auction catalog. Catalog subscribers will then be able to bid on your items, and you get a check minus a 15% commission plus a subscription/processing fee.

http://www.onlineauction.com

Onlineauction.com is mainly collectibles, with links to collector's resources and price guides. The site features something called "Snipe-IT-Bid auctions, where with a single click you can advance the high bid to the next highest increment.

http://www.reverseauction.com

While they don't feature antiques and collectibles, if you're looking for something different in an online auction how about watching the bid price of an item *decrease* over time! At reverseauction.com that is just what happens, and the first person to place a bid wins the auction. The challenge is in not waiting too long for the price to go lower or someone else will beat you to it.

http://www.seriouscollector.com

Serious Collector is a learning, communication, and trading site that includes retail sales, auctions, resources such as current news and articles, free online shops, links to Web resources, and collector forums.

http://auctions.yahoo.com

Yahoo! is free to registered users for both buying and selling, and has recently expanded their services to include a search for items near where you live (helpful for those large furniture purchases that you can pick up), a featured auctions category, bold type listings, and a customized listings page you can create using your own logo and photos.

http://www.cyrbid.com

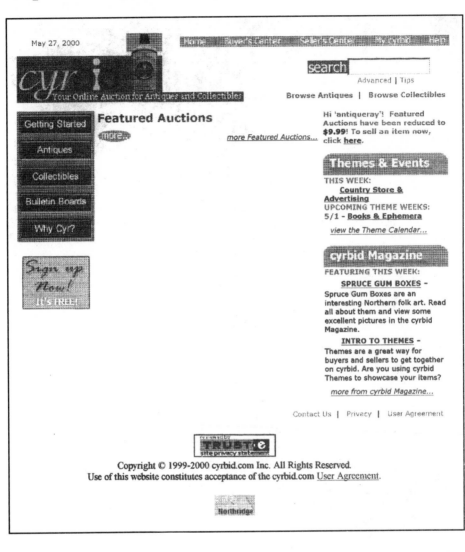

search
Advanced | Tips

Browse Antiques | Browse Collectibles

Getting Started
Antiques
Collectibles
Bulletin Boards
Why Cyr?

Sign up Now!
It's FREE!

Featured Auctions

more

more Featured Auctions...

Hi 'antiqueray'! Featured Auctions have been reduced to **$9.99**! To sell an item now, click **here**.

Themes & Events

THIS WEEK:
Country Store & Advertising
UPCOMING THEME WEEKS:
5/1 - **Books & Ephemera**

view the Theme Calendar...

cyrbid Magazine

FEATURING THIS WEEK:

SPRUCE GUM BOXES –
Spruce Gum Boxes are an interesting Northern folk art. Read all about them and view some excellent pictures in the cyrbid Magazine.

INTRO TO THEMES –
Themes are a great way for buyers and sellers to get together on cyrbid. Are you using cyrbid Themes to showcase your items?

more from cyrbid Magazine...

Contact Us | Privacy | User Agreement

reviewed by
TRUST e
site privacy statement

Northridge

http://www.ehammer.com

Create Auction | Search | My Info   Sitemap | Help | Auction Galleries

THE ON-LINE AUCTION OF

Auction Categories

ANTIQUES & COLLECTIBLES

American Antiques
British and European Antiques
Asian Antiques
Artwork and Prints
Collectibles
Comic Books and Art
Ephemera
Photography
Pottery and Porcelain
Toys
Jewelry
more....

Welcome to eHammer

Search for Keywords:

[   ] [Search]

Picture Your Ad Here...

WHAT'S HOT

REGISTER TO BUY & SELL

MANAGE YOUR ACCOUNT

AUCTION GALLERIES

SELL AN ITEM

Premier Auctions

Incredible Mahjong Set in Carved Case

!!LG. HERIZ ORIENTAL RUG RUGTIME MEMORIAL DAY $$

EARLY Miniature on Ivory-Man with TOP HAT!

Early Pair of Architectural Columns-GREAT PAINT!

HANDEL lamp-Reverse Painted Shade

Beautiful FULPER BOWL with frog

RARE BOOK-Grandma Moses-MY LIFE'S HISTORY-SIGNED

Historic Stamps of America Collection

antique percussion derringer black power

antique percussion derringer black power

New **Bulk Uploading**

eHammer Sponsored Charity Auctions

RUG ANTIQUES

This Month's Featured Auction Gallery

http://auctions.excite.com

 **Brand Names, Bargains & Collectibles**

fairmarket NETWORK

My Excite | Check Email

Sign-In

Auctions Home   Advanced Search   Sell an Item   My Account   Help

Search Auctions: [_____]   Search

GETTING STARTED

- Register Now
- Auction Overview
- How Do I Bid?
- How Do I Sell?
  Free Listings!

Clearance Items and Hot Collectibles

New Auction!
Computer Equipment
Starting At $1!

Bid Now For
Your Chance To
Win $10,000!

Outdoor Gear!
Lanterns, Jackets,
Sweaters, Blankets...

Don't Miss Out!
- New Listings
- Items in Your Area
- One Hour Left

Auction Shops

Bid for items on sale by brand name merchants.

10k BidStakes!

WIN $10,000 each weekday! Just place a bid and you're entered.

More Places to Buy

- Classifieds
- Excite Shopping

Browse by Category

Art & Antiques 6,055
Antiques, Prints, Sculptures...

Books & Magazines 3,341
Fiction, Non-Fiction, Magazines...

Clothing 2,286
Men's Apparel, Women's Casual......

Coins & Stamps 3,311
U.S. Coins, U.S. Stamps...

Collectibles 29,570
Autographs, Holiday, Comics...

Computers & Software 21,142
Desktops, Laptops, Printers...

Electronics & Photo 4,093
Photography, Stereo, Video...

Home & Garden 6,634
Housewares, Furnishings...

Jewelry 15,748
Women's Rings, Other Gold...

Music & Movies 8,503
CD's, Movies...

Office 422
Supplies, Furniture...

Other Goods & Services 2,606
Accessories, Gifts, Hobbies...

Porcelain & Glass 2,996
Glass, Porcelain, Pottery...

Sports & Recreation 1,693
Cycling, Golf...

Sports Memorabilia 6,792
Autographs, Trading Cards...

Toys & Hobbies 9,542
Beanies, Diecast, Dolls, Pokemon...

Travel & Tickets 1,511
Air Travel, Vacation Packages...

Vehicles 763
Accessories, Classic Cars...

View all categories

http://www.haggle.com

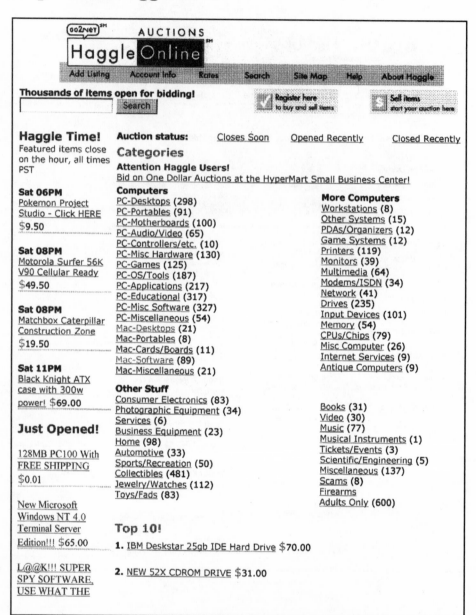

Thousands of items open for bidding! [Search]

Register here to buy and sell items

Sell items start your auction here

Haggle Time!
Featured items close on the hour, all times PST

Auction status: Closes Soon   Opened Recently   Closed Recently

Categories

Attention Haggle Users!
Bid on One Dollar Auctions at the HyperMart Small Business Center!

Sat 06PM
Pokemon Project Studio - Click HERE
$9.50

Sat 08PM
Motorola Surfer 56K V90 Cellular Ready
$49.50

Sat 08PM
Matchbox Caterpillar Construction Zone
$19.50

Sat 11PM
Black Knight ATX case with 300w power! $69.00

Just Opened!

128MB PC100 With FREE SHIPPING
$0.01

New Microsoft Windows NT 4.0 Terminal Server Edition!!! $65.00

L@@K!!! SUPER SPY SOFTWARE, USE WHAT THE

Computers
PC-Desktops (298)
PC-Portables (91)
PC-Motherboards (100)
PC-Audio/Video (65)
PC-Controllers/etc. (10)
PC-Misc Hardware (130)
PC-Games (125)
PC-OS/Tools (187)
PC-Applications (217)
PC-Educational (317)
PC-Misc Software (327)
PC-Miscellaneous (54)
Mac-Desktops (21)
Mac-Portables (8)
Mac-Cards/Boards (11)
Mac-Software (89)
Mac-Miscellaneous (21)

Other Stuff
Consumer Electronics (83)
Photographic Equipment (34)
Services (6)
Business Equipment (23)
Home (98)
Automotive (33)
Sports/Recreation (50)
Collectibles (481)
Jewelry/Watches (112)
Toys/Fads (83)

More Computers
Workstations (8)
Other Systems (15)
PDAs/Organizers (12)
Game Systems (12)
Printers (119)
Monitors (39)
Multimedia (64)
Modems/ISDN (34)
Network (41)
Drives (235)
Input Devices (101)
Memory (54)
CPUs/Chips (79)
Misc Computer (26)
Internet Services (9)
Antique Computers (9)

Books (31)
Video (30)
Music (77)
Musical Instruments (1)
Tickets/Events (3)
Scientific/Engineering (5)
Miscellaneous (137)
Scams (8)
Firearms
Adults Only (600)

Top 10!

1. IBM Deskstar 25gb IDE Hard Drive $70.00

2. NEW 52X CDROM DRIVE $31.00

http://www.kaleden.com

WWW.KALEDEN.COM *welcome page* | help | feedback | about kaleden | co

site navigation

MALLS NETWORK

DEALERS NETWORK

MALLS DIRECTORY

ALL AUCTIONS

PRICE GUIDE

CALENDARS

ONLINE PUBLICATIONS

REGISTER

ALL CATEGORIES

NEWS

PRESS RELEASES

FORUMS

ON THIS DAY

LINKS

SITE RULES

POWER SEARCH

SEARCH

publications

American Antiquities Journal

Antique Traveller

Antiques & Collecting Magazine

Antiques Magazine

AntiqueWeek

Carter's Homes, Antiques & Collectibles

Collectors News

Great Lakes Trader

Old Stuff

Orientations

Southern Antiques

The Daze

ᴴᴼᵂ ᵀᴼ join **ᴴᴼᵂ ᵀᴼ buy** **ᴴᴼᵂ ᵀᴼ sell** | User Name: [ ] Log In! | Password: [ ]

BARGAIN AUCTIONS STARTING AT $1

Wedgwood vase - This Wedgewood vase is in Jasper blue and dates back to 1974. It is 7 3/4" tall. There are no chips...
Closes:May 30, 2000 12:00 PM EST (2 days, 14 hours)
Highest bid: $11.00 by MillerRon bid history

Roseville Rosecraft bowl - This Roseville Rosecraft vintage closed bowl is 5"X3"- The ornamentation on the side is that of grap...
Closes:May 30, 2000 12:00 PM EST (2 days, 14 hours)
Highest bid: $7.00 by brigadier bid history

Japanese bronze box - This Japanese bronze box is of the type made in the late 19th century, after the Meiji restoration o...
Closes:May 30, 2000 12:00 PM EST (2 days, 14 hours)
Highest bid: $14.00 by brigadier bid history

FEATURED SALES

Gold Earrings
18 karat gold earrings set with 170 diamonds 3.40 carats total, and 72 invisible set sapphires
For sale in D.S. Clarke World Famous Miami Antique Show by Blythe Jewelers, priced $2,900.00

Cast iron toy
Early cast iron horse & dump cart. Original colors: green, red, black, white. Sand & Gravel stamped ...
For sale in Mollyockett Marketplace Antique Center by Belskis Antiques, priced $225.00

Old Ivory Cake Plate
This Silesia Old Ivory China double-handled cake plate is in the #200 pattern. In the art deco style...
For sale in Mollyockett Marketplace Antique Center by Kimberly Poland Antiques, priced $125.00

SITE NEWS

05.17.00 Starting May 23, Auction Dollar Days at Kaleden.com - Minimum bid$1 - No Reserve. Come one - come all to Kaleden.com's Auction Dollar

items for sale

Advertising (179)

Ancient World (7)

Antiques, General (424)

Arts (274)

Books and Magazines (130)

Ceramics (3811)

Coins and Stamps (4)

Collectibles, General (298)

Collector's Editions (298)

Desirables (21)

Dolls (116)

Electronics and Business Machines (18)

Furniture (372)

Glass (1971)

House and Garden (1246)

Jewelry (505)

Metals (428)

Militaria (132)

Miscellaneous (668)

Oriental Arts (415)

Paper (471)

Rocks and Minerals (1)

Sports Memorabilia (49)

Textiles (286)

Toys and Games (193)

Transportation (21)

http://www.manions.com

Post Auction
212

Sign Up On-line
Coming Soon

Post Auction 212 orders must be phoned, faxed or e-mailed in by June 15, 2000.
This is a first come, first served bases.

Auction 212 is now Closed.

Our Auction items are grouped by catalog. Select the one of your interest below:

Members

About Us

Subscribe!

Auction
Schedule

Guidelines

Show
Schedule

Contact Us

Log Off

**Antiques &
Collectibles**

**U.S. Historical
Collectibles**

**German
Historical
Collectibles**

**Japanese &
Other
Countries**

Firearms

**Trendline New
& Retail Sales**

Over 20,000 items available every 6 weeks!

Hot German Specials

Special Collection in 212 Auction

Click below to sample some items.

- U.S. Uniforms
- Dolls
- Japanese Swords
- Pistols

- US Army Knives
- Lighters
- Toys
- German Helmets

- Blue Jeans
- German Medals
- Third Reich
- German Uniforms

- FYI (For Your Information!) Consignor Information Page click here...
- HOW TO BID ONLINE!! Bidding Info, Online Bidding how-to, etc. click here...
- COOKIES, COOKIES, COOKIES!! Do you get an error every time you click on an item to see more detail or bid? Your web browser must have "cookies" turned on. click here...
- HOT NEWS!! **The True Virtual Auction!**
  for more information about 10 minute bidding click here...

http://www.onlineauction.com

 Online auction

Browse | Sell | O-mail | Help | Search | Auction Manager
Home   Register   Secure User   News   Chat   Site Map

Hot Categories

Collectibles (736)
Trading Cards (452)
Memorabilia (400)
Miscellaneous (188)
Jewelry & Gemstones (185)
Comic Books (125)
Art (112)
Antiques (105)
Home Accessories (87)
Glass (67)
Porcelain (50)
all categories...

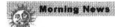 **Morning News**

Latest News Article
French Court Pushes Bounds on Yahoo Ruling

Latest Press Release
Onlineauction.com Teams Up!

Resource Links

Price Guides, Cyber Malls
World News, Stocks, Health
Free PC Stuff, Music, more...

Onlineauction.com will be giving away a 1978 Anniversary Model Corvette. A public drawing will be held Sunday July 16th at the Portland Expo.

[Search] Search Tips

This item Selling at
ABSOLUTE AUCTION
No Minimum - No Reserve
More ...**view ALL Absolute Auctions**

Featured Auctions

49ER ADJUSTABLE CAP ~ NFL Team Hat ~ NR

Beautiful Sterling Floating Heart with Chain

New Gold & Blue Renaissance Dagger/Knife C@@L

STUNNING Depression BLOCK OPTIC Place Settings (4)

EXQUISITE CS PRUSSIA Dessert Set

Large Elegant Glass Etched Bowl MINT! N/R
More ...**view ALL Featured Auctions**

Hot Auction Items

LARGE WHITE ROSE HEAVY BAKED ENAMEL GAS SIGN

"BATMAN" First Draft Screenplay

Original Coca-Cola Wall Sign #4 NO RESERVE!

Circa 1950s Coca-Cola Clock NO RESERVE!

Mark McGwire 1988 Topps League Leaders (REVCO) ÜÜ

Mark McGwire 1995 SP SILVER (RARE) ÜÜ

Advertise With Us!

Learning Center

Register, It's free!
How do I bid?
How do I sell?
What is O-mail?
O-lister Download it!

Shows & Events

Kool Stuff

The
Best Stuff
in the
Free World

What's New!

Buyer's Assurance
Automatic Feedback
Snipe-IT-Bid
Site Announcements

30 Day Stats

33490 Items Listed
$84909.10 in bids received
870669 Avg page Views

Online auction, Online auction, Online auction, online auction, online auction, online auction

escrow.com

59

http://www.reverseauction.com

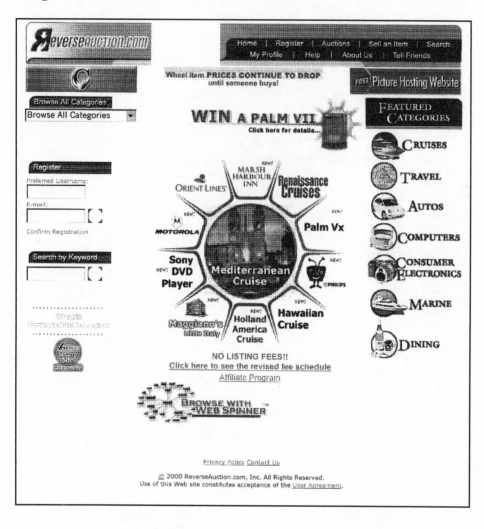

Market **Auctions** **Forums**
Resources **News** **Members**

Join Today,
It's
Free!

Main Categories

Antiques
Architecture & Design
Books & Manuscripts
Ephemera & Advertising
Fine & Graphic Arts
Folk & Ethnographic Art
Jewelry & Silver
Machines & Coin-Op
Maps & Globes
Memorabilia & Autographs
Militaria, Arms & Armor
Music & Instruments
Other & Miscellaneous
Philately, Numismatics & c.
Photography & Optical
Porcelain, Pottery, & Glass
Timepieces
Tools & Services
Toys, Puzzles, & Hobbies

(View all)

Serious Search

Search! | **Go!** Advanced

Search our online catalog of 50,000+ listings of merchandise, resources, and auctions, and 185+ dealers.

Featured Member

The Philadelphia Print Shop, Ltd. (Philadelphia, PA) is among the world's largest dealers of antique maps, prints, and related books and reference materials. The Philadelphia Print Shop specializes in the American theme.(visit)

Featured Listing

Henning and Nancy Kramer, owners of Sparrows Inc. (Kensington, MD) offer quality French antiques to the American market. This French marble by Carpeaux, '*Le Rieur Napolitain*' circa 1880, typifies the Kramers' emphasis on quality and beauty. (more)

www.SeriousCollector.com

The Online Community for Serious Collectors and Professionals in Fine Arts, Antiques, and Enduring Collectibles.

What's New? The News!

Member Entrance

What is the Serious Collector?

Dealers: Open Your Free Online Store Today!

Newest Inventory

Newest Members

Newest Messages

DEALERS:
Create Your Free Online Shop in Minutes!

Notify Me!

Become a Serious Collector - It's Free

Want Ads

Appraisal Forum

Newest Resources

VeriSign

AR Antique Resources Awards

San Francisco Chronicle

TRUST·e
site privacy statement

http://auctions.yahoo.com

N'Sync vs. Backstreet Boys on Yahoo! Auctions

Welcome, Guest

Submit Item - View Alerts - My Auctions - Options - Sign in

Yahoo! Auctions

Getting Started

- How to Bid
- How to Sell
- Auctions Tour
- What's New ??

You are not signed in
You must sign in to bid or sell.

Yahoo! ID: [ ]

Yahoo! Password [ ]

☐ Remember my ID & Password

 Sign in

New User?
Sign Up Here

Featured Site

B2B Marketplace

Search Business to Business Products

Charity Auctions

Bid on authentic Lance Armstrong cycling shoes to support the Lance Armstrong Foundation

Other Charity Auctions

- Actors' Fund
- Nylon Magazine

Selected Auctions in Lincoln Cents

1909 VDB Lincoln Cent XF

1865 Three-Cent Piece (AG) - N/R!

1909-S Lincoln Head Cent - VG

Find Auctions

[ ] Search Advanced

Antiques & Collectibles *(382,849)*
Numismatics, Memorabilia, Advertising...

Home & Garden *(63,180)*
Housewares, Baby Items, Furnishings...

Arts & Entertainment *(370,009)*
Books, Music, Movies...

Sports & Recreation *(95,488)*
Sporting Goods, Tickets, Hobbies & Crafts...

Business & Office *(5,457)*
Furniture, Business Machines...

Toys & Games *(295,618)*
Video Games, Pokemon, Beanie Babies@...

Clothing & Accessories *(148,150)*
Jewelry, Women's, Men's...

Trading Cards *(435,300)*
Baseball, Football, Games@...

Computers *(69,228)*
Hardware, Software, Domain Names...

Travel & Transportation *(22,065)*
Travel Tickets, Automotive...

Electronics & Cameras *(21,006)*
Audio, Video, Cameras & Equipment...

Other Goods & Services *(52,322)*
Health & Beauty, Flowers, Real Estate...

Full Category Index...

International Auctions

Europe : Denmark - France - Germany - Italy - Spain - Sweden - UK & Ireland
Pacific Rim : Australia & NZ - Hong Kong - Japan - Korea - Singapore - Taiwan
Americas : Brazil - Canada - Mexico

Success Stories (Add Mine)

ITEM-SPECIFIC AUCTIONS

Specializing in certain items is not a new concept, and some of the online auction sites are doing it with success. Here is a sampling of a few...

http://www.auctionvine.com

Are fine and rare wines your weakness? Pay a visit to Auction Vine and acquire a bottle of Chateau Lynch-Bages Vintage 1961. French wines are usually readily available, if you're willing to pay the price.

http://www.justglass.com

Just glass is just that—glassware. From art glass to Fire King, you'll find it here along with an online magazine with useful glass facts written by respected authorities, a reference library available to members with prices realized from both conventional and online auctions as well as shows and retail sales, and online shops where you can buy glassware in a retail environment instead of bidding.

http://www.potteryauction.com

Point your browser here for free listings, no commissions, no buyer's fee, and free image hosting along with a selection of items from most of the well-known names in pottery making.

http://www.auctionvine.com

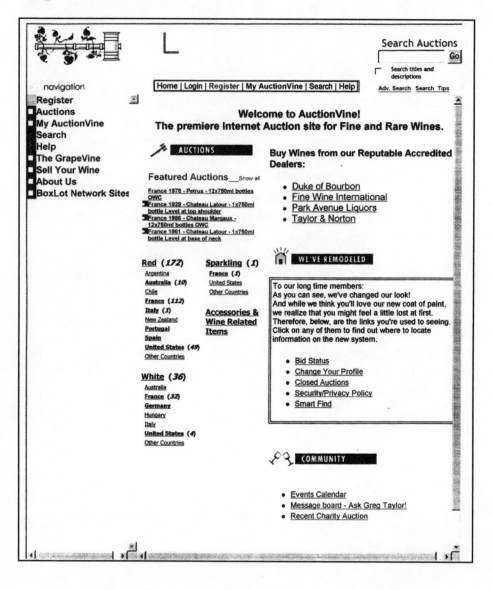

navigation
- Register
- Auctions
- My AuctionVine
- Search
- Help
- The GrapeVine
- Sell Your Wine
- About Us
- BoxLot Network Sites

Home | Login | Register | My AuctionVine | Search | Help

Search Auctions

Go

☐ Search titles and descriptions

Adv. Search   Search Tips

Welcome to AuctionVine!
The premiere Internet Auction site for Fine and Rare Wines.

AUCTIONS

Featured Auctions __Show all

- France 1978 - Petrus - 12x750ml bottles OWC
- France 1929 - Chateau Latour - 1x750ml bottle Level at top shoulder
- France 1986 - Chateau Margaux - 12x750ml bottles OWC
- France 1961 - Chateau Latour - 1x750ml bottle Level at base of neck

Red (172)
- Argentina
- Australia (10)
- Chile
- France (112)
- Italy (1)
- New Zealand
- Portugal
- Spain
- United States (49)
- Other Countries

White (36)
- Australia
- France (32)
- Germany
- Hungary
- Italy
- United States (4)
- Other Countries

Sparkling (1)
- France (1)
- United States
- Other Countries

Accessories & Wine Related Items

Buy Wines from our Reputable Accredited Dealers:

- Duke of Bourbon
- Fine Wine International
- Park Avenue Liquors
- Taylor & Norton

WE'VE REMODELED

To our long time members:
As you can see, we've changed our look!
And while we think you'll love our new coat of paint,
we realize that you might feel a little lost at first.
Therefore, below, are the links you're used to seeing.
Click on any of them to find out where to locate
information on the new system.

- Bid Status
- Change Your Profile
- Closed Auctions
- Security/Privacy Policy
- Smart Find

COMMUNITY

- Events Calendar
- Message board - Ask Greg Taylor!
- Recent Charity Auction

No Listing Fees or Commissions

@ JUST GLASS

Welcome
About Us
News Events
Press Releases
Site Map
FAQ's

Online Magazine

RESOURCES

Online magazine
Reference Library
Dealer Shops
The Bookstore
Advertise

CONNECTIONS

Do You ICQ?

Play a Game?

"Ask Tiffy..."

Join Our IE
Channel
Send an Online

CATEGORIES

Akro Agate/Marbles *(1)*

Ancient Glass *(8)*
Art Glass *(383)*
American *(110)*
Bohemian *(16)*
Czech *(18)*
English *(21)*
French *(56)*
General *(127)*
Italian *(31)*
Scandinavian *(2)*

Avon *(11)*

Barware *(45)*

Boyd Glass *(8)*

Carnival Glass *(133)*
Contemporary Carnival *(30)*
General *(10)*
Vintage Carnival *(93)*

Character/Premium
Glasses *(18)*

Coll. 40's, 50's, 60's Glass
(160)

Contemporary Glass (1970
- Present) *(42)*

Crystal *(302)*

Custard Glass *(1)*

Cut Glass *(72)*

Depression Glass *(331)*

Duncan & Miller *(33)*
Fostoria *(101)*
General *(75)*
Heisey *(36)*
Imperial *(23)*
Tiffin *(15)*

Fenton *(155)*

Fire-King / Anchor
Hocking *(120)*

Glass Animals *(48)*

Glass Beads *(3)*

Glass Bottles *(24)*

Glass Jewelry *(41)*

Glass Paper/Books
(66)

Glass Shoes *(5)*

Kitchen Glass *(38)*

Lamps / Lighting *(17)*

Milk Glass *(67)*

Misc. Glass *(126)*

Mosser Glass *(6)*

New Glass *(25)*

Opalescent Glass *(34)*

Paperweights *(75)*

http://www.potteryauction.com

ONLINE MALLS

In addition, there are sites where merchandise is for sale by a set price rather than in an auction environment. Some of these sites also deserve your attention.

Elegant Antique Mall
http://www.elegantantiques.com

Elegant Antique Mall offers a selection of antiques and collectibles in online antique dealer booths, with an emphasis on glassware and pottery.

AntiqueArts.com
http://www.antiquearts.com

Over 100 independent dealers, most with an online catalog, and a search engine to help you locate what you're looking for.

collect.com
http://www.collect.com

Collect.com has evolved into a thriving online community, with thousands of items offered by hundreds of merchants as well as online price guides, reference materials, and classified ads.

Collector Online
http://www.collectoronline.com

A major Internet mall with items from over 200 different dealers. An innovative online Inventory Management System (IMS) allows you to catalog an unlimited number of items and send them to eBay™, Auction Universe, Yahoo! Auctions, or your Collector Online booth with the click of a mouse.

Ruby Lane
http://www.rubylane.com

An excellent antiques and collectibles search engine, as well as a place to build your free online storefront and display your merchandise for sale.

The Internet Antique Store
http://www.tias.com

One of the largest antiques and collectibles malls on the Internet. Over 220,000 listings and a site search engine make shopping fun and easy.

INDIVIDUAL DEALERS

A great selection of antiques and collectibles are available online from an ever-increasing number of individual dealers.

A-Mark Precious Metals
http://www.amark.com

Since its founding in 1965, A-Mark has grown into a firm with annual sales exceeding $1 billion and is a full service precious metal trading company offering a wide array of products and services. Daily prices are posted for gold, silver and other precious metals.

Antique Cupboard
http://www.antiquecupboard.com

At Antique Cupboard you'll find sterling, sterling, and more sterling including Jensen, Tiffany, and entire sets. They also stock a nice selection of collector plates.

Hakes Americana & Collectibles
http://www.hakes.com

Hakes mail order auctions are well known in the collectibles trade, and have expanded to include internet auction listings. Some of the same items that go up for bid are also available online to buy immediately at fixed prices.

D'Antiques Limited
http://www.dantiques.com

Don't be fooled by the D'Antiques claim of being the premiere virtual junk store on the Web—they have some fine antiques and collectibles too.

Durwyn Smedley Antiques
http://www.smedley.com

Modern design movements of the 20th Century including Arts & Crafts, Art Deco, and Mid-Century Modern. Art pottery and tiles, American designer dinnerware.

Funk and Junk
http://www.funkandjunk.com

Character glasses, action figures, five-and-dime items, political items, vintage clothing, and much more including categories by decades (1950s, 1970's, etc.).

Old Orchard Antiques
http://www.oldorchardantiques.com
A selection of advertising, ephemera, jewelry, glass, pottery, and toys coupled with friendly, efficient service makes this a site to bookmark.

Southampton Antiques
(http://www.souhantq.com)
Based in Massachusetts, Southampton has a wonderful selection of fine quality antiques. Their Web site is well designed, attractive, easy to navigate, and contains some great New England finds.

CLASSIFIED ADS
Selling antiques and collectibles through Internet classified ads is becoming more common. Most are free—you can't beat that price!

ForSale.com
http://www.forsale.com
ForSale.com specializes in classified listings for everything from antiques and collectibles to computers. Registration is free and once registered you can place and edit your ads. You can also create your own free storefront from this site.

INFORMATION DIRECTORIES
Looking for links to other antiques and collectibles sites, price guides, and reference books? Look no further.

Antique Hot Spots
http://www.antiquehotspots.com
A directory of hundreds of antique and collectibles sites with links to them from one location. Search for relevant sites by using keywords, or simply click on a letter for an alphabetic listing of sites to browse.

Antique Networking
http://www.antiqnet.com
Many links to both malls and individual dealer shops as well as information on shows, publications, insurance, and a host of other useful related information.

Curioscape
http://www.curioscape.com

Curioscape is an extensive directory of links to specific categories, including art, coins, dolls, glassware, and many more.

Collector Link (Cards)
http://www.collector-link.com

Links to Web sites and news groups for card magazines and price guides, card issuers, dealers and private collectors.

ShopNow.com
http://www.shopnow.com

While this is a site that lists stores of all descriptions, not just antiques and collectibles, all you have to do is type "antiques" or "collectibles" into the Easy-Search box on their home page, click "Go", and get a list of links to more fun places to explore.

World Collectors Net
http://www.worldcollectorsnet.com

A site for collectibles, featuring a shopping arcade, information pages, articles, reviews, message boards, price guides, a bookstore and a swap shop all under one virtual roof.

ONLINE PRICE GUIDES
Kovels'
http://www.kovels.com

Well-known antique and collectible researchers Ralph and Terry Kovel share their knowledge with current news articles and an expansive general online price guide. Site registration is free, and entitles you to get 50 prices from their price guide. The good news is that after you use those fifty you will be awarded with 50 more free searches—the 50 search option seems to be perpetually renewable at this time.

Antique Trader Price Guide
http://www.collect.com/priceguide

Antique Trader also has a general online price guide containing all of the information from their 1995-2000 annual paperback editions, and unlimited access is available for $15.95 per year. Alternately, you can purchase the printed paperback price guide and get free access to the online version for specified period of time, also for $15.95.

OnlinePriceguide.com
http://www.online-priceguide.com

OnlinePriceguide.com features over one million free real world prices in their database, as well as additional databases available on a fee basis.

Slawinski Auction Company
http://www.slawinski.com

A price guide for Victorian furniture and a few other miscellaneous categories is available at *http://www.slawinski.com*. Slawinski is an auction company that is posting actual auction results on their Web site in the form of a price guide. This is not only a creative form of advertising, but could eventually lead to an invaluable source of price information available at your fingertips if other auctioneers see value in it.

Art*fact*
http://www.artfact.com

Art*fact* is a subscription based online price guide available to art and antiques professionals. ArtFact Incorporated was founded in 1989 with the charter of providing the highest quality independent public auction information to serious professionals within the art and antiques world. The database, comprised of art, antiques, collectibles, and jewelry, has grown to over four million entries, and many of the most prestigious auction houses in the world contribute the information.

Alleyguide.com
http://www.alleyguide.com

If you're into diecast cars like Matchbox, Hot Wheels, or Johnny Lightning, visit *http://www.alleyguide.com* for an extensive price guide of these items.

Roycroft Copper
http://www.roycroftcopper.com

Arts and Crafts collectors of Roycroft copper can get estimated current market values of select pieces as well as photos and descriptions.

PEZ Dispensers
http://www.pezheads.org

PEZ dispensers have their own online price guide on the Internet, with over 600 photos updated daily.

Steiff Collectibles
http://www.collectorvalues.com

Values for more than 6,000 Steiff collectibles can be accessed from here by typing a Steiff EAN# or keyword, like "bear", into the search box.

eBay™
http://www.ebay.com

What's that? I thought eBay™ was an auction site. It is, but it also can serve as a very effective tool to determine what prices the market will bear on a large variety of items. With over four million items up for sale at any given time, and an option to run a search among auctions completed in the past 30 days, you in essence have an extensive database of information for prices realized.

Go to *http://www.ebay.com* and click on the **Search** box at the top of the page. Once on the search page, click the **Complete Auctions** tab. Type a keyword or two into the box and your instant electronic price guide appears before your eyes.

Let's say you came across a nice flue cover at your local flea market that the seller thought was just a print in a metal frame and priced it at $8.00. You knew enough to buy it, but didn't have a good idea of value. Using the eBay™ completed auction feature, you could run a search using the keywords "flue cover"—I did just that and had a database of 169 items to evaluate at my convenience, complete with final auction values. While you may not find an exact match for your item, especially if it's not a mass produced collectible, you can get a pretty good feel as to what your particular piece is worth. And if you *are* dealing in mass marketed collectibles, you may well come up with many listings giving prices for the exact item you have. You might be surprised at how often the prices realized for identical items are within a few dollars of each other. Instant fair market value!

An art nouveau brass
picture frame.

Celebrity
collectibles: a
"Beutebox" by
CANCO and a
film magazine
honoring
1920's movie
star Betty
Compson.

Mission-style lamp with a mica shade.

A Seth Thomas Adamantine clock from the 1880s.

Chapter 5
Using eBay™, the
Granddaddy of the Online Auctions

We've finally arrived! This chapter will walk you through the process of registering and using eBay™, the world's largest online auction. I'll stay basic here but give you some advanced tips in Chapter 7. Once you've mastered the skills associated with using eBay™ you can visit any auction you'd like—they all work very similarly.

The functions described in this chapter can be accessed from eBay™'s home page (**www.ebay.com**) or once you're inside the eBay™ community from the menu at the top of each screen. If you're having trouble finding a particular area within eBay™ click Site Map on the menu and you'll have access to links from all areas of the eBay™ community. So let's GO!

Register

If you're 18 years of age or older and have a permanent address and e-mail account you can register to use eBay™. Registration is a process that requires submitting (online, of course) some basic information and receiving back a confirmation number via e-mail. You then confirm your registration by accepting eBay's™ User Agreement and choosing a screen name and password (do NOT use the confirmation number eBay™ sent to you for a password). This information is again submitted online, along with the original confirmation number supplied by eBay™, and your registration is complete. eBay™ does a good job of walking you through the process, making it very easy. In fact the hardest part is figuring out what you want to call yourself (your eBay™ screen name) and choosing a password. Don't forget that password! It's your ticket to the eBay™ community.

Registration is a one-time occurrence and once confirmed you may sell or buy as much as you'd like without doing it again. Depending on the volume of users the wait to get your confirmation e-mail might take hours or perhaps a day, so if you register and want to bid right away you may be disappointed. But while you're waiting for your confirmation e-mail you can browse the listings and get familiar with the auction community in general.

You will notice that eBay™ gives you the option of registering using *SSL*. SSL stands for Secure Sockets Layer and is a technology developed by Netscape (don't panic—it works with Microsoft Internet Explorer too) as a more secure way of sending information over the Internet. While the registration process does not require you to give any more information than is already available in public records, I recommend you always use SSL when available for any Internet transactions. Online privacy will become more of an issue, and you should get in the habit of using any means available to protect yours.

To register using SSL, simply click the box as instructed on the eBay Registration screen and then click the "Begin registration process now" bar. A popup box will appear telling that you are about to view pages over a secure connection. Click OK and you will proceed to the secure registration site. Check the address bar at the top of your browser window— if it starts with https:// instead of http:// you are on a secure site. Another way to verify you're secure is to check for an icon in the lower right part of your browser window that looks like a locked padlock.

BUYERS

Other than the money you'll owe the seller when purchasing an item, buying on eBay™ is free. There are no fees to pay as there are when listing an item for sale.

Browsing the Listings

If you're not looking for anything in particular (if you are see Search listings later in this chapter) you can browse through thousands of listings and most assuredly find something of interest to you. eBay™ is split into over 2,000 categories, and while this alone sounds intimidating it makes browsing much easier than if everything was together. You can choose categories from Antiques to Computers to Jewelry. Once you select a category you can refine even more; for instance Antiques lets you choose Ancient World, Books & Manuscripts, Folk Art, and others. Click on a category and the listings appear before you, ready for you to place your bids!

Browsing the Listings

home | my eBay | site map | sign in

Browse | Sell | Services | Search | Help | Community

categories | featured | hot | grab bag | great gifts | big ticket

SEARCH

tips | All eBay Regions ▼

☐ Search only in **Collectibles**
☐ Search titles **and** descriptions

Kitchenware (40359)
General (12604)
Cookie Cutters (1042)
Cookie Jars (3664)
Cookware (2872)
Graniteware (1700)
Open Salts (861)
Salt, Pepper Shakers (9550)
Small Appliances (1924)
Tableware (4029)
Utensils (2113)

Knives (13968)
General (8385)
Commemorative (806)
Pocket (4777)

Lamps (10198)
General (1137)
Candle Holders (771)
Electric (4421)
Non Electric (2361)
Parts (637)
Shades (871)

Limited Editions (2494)

Locks, Keys (1019)

Lunchboxes (3029)
General (516)
Metal (1946)
Plastic (419)
Vintage (148)

Advertising (100147)
General (9489)
Airlines (3437)
Auto (17716)
Bakery (534)
Bus (173)
Candy (2895)
Cereal (1209)
Character (1555)
Cigarette (2646)
Clocks (321)
Coffee (934)
Dairy (2527)
Displays (466)
Distillery (4190)
Dolls (178)
Drug Store (1298)
Farm (4008)
Fashion (457)
Food (2380)
Forest Service (213)
Gasoline (7292)
General Store (770)
Household (1184)
Labels (1885)
Mr. Peanut (508)
Premiums (1091)
Radio/Phonograph (888)
Restaurant (1197)
Seed, Feed (501)

Chat about Advertising; Elvis with other eBay members

Avoid post office lines. Get 50% off the E-Stamp Starter Kit!

greAt colleCtions

Visit eBay Great Collections for guaranteed collectibles from auction houses and dealers.

featured auctions

See all featured auctions in this category....

special events

NEW! Billpoint, buy and sell with a credit card. Fast, Easy, Secure!

Time to shop for Timepieces on eBay.

Come see eBay's NEW Virtual Antique Mall.

New! Toon in to Comics-O-rama.

Journey to another dimension— Sci-Fi-O-rama!

front page

The summer festival that collectors will want to attend is Beaglefest in Santa Rosa, California, eBay Magazine reports. The late Charles Schulz and the Peanuts gang will be feted.

Viewing a Listing

Scroll through the myriad of listings in your category and find one that sounds interesting to you. If it has a green icon that looks like a camera in front of it you're in luck—the seller has supplied a photo of the merchandise. But don't be deterred (yet) if it doesn't—sellers use different methods of listing and, particularly when they have more than one photo to post, don't always get the camera icon to appear. So click on the listing that interests you and hope a photo is there. If it's not, I recommend you refrain from bidding (see Chapter 8—Protecting Yourself from Internet Auction Fraud).

What appears before you now is a screen showing some information about the seller, the current high bid amount for this auction, the high bidder's screen name and the time left before the auction expires. By scrolling down you come upon a description of the merchandise and hopefully a photo or two. Scrolling even further you're in the bid area where you can specify the amount you'd like to bid on this merchandise. The minimum acceptable bid is also displayed here.

Search Listings

While the Internet has search engines that spread across the World Wide Web, some online auctions have engines that search their sites specifically. These are invaluable when browsing a large auction site such as eBay™ for a particular item or item group. For instance a search of eBay™ on May 27, 2000 at 7:00 a.m. EST for listings containing the words "Roy Rogers" yielded no less than 1217 entries! (As an interesting aside, the same search during the production of the first edition of this book produced 377 entries and for the 2nd edition 951—eBay™ has indeed grown!) Belt buckles, autographs, posters, and just about anything else having to do with "Roy Rogers" is available to be bought—all at the same auction. You can now assemble a collection in less than a week that would have taken years and possibly a lifetime before. Does this take the fun out of collecting? Absolutely not, as you'll find out when your heart is pounding as you wait to see if your final bid on an item you've always wanted holds up in the final minutes.

eBay™ provides a number of useful search programs. You can search for items by title, items listed by a particular seller, items you (or any other bidder) has bid on recently, or by the number eBay™ assigns each listing. The one you will use the most, at least in the beginning, is by title.

Viewing a Listing

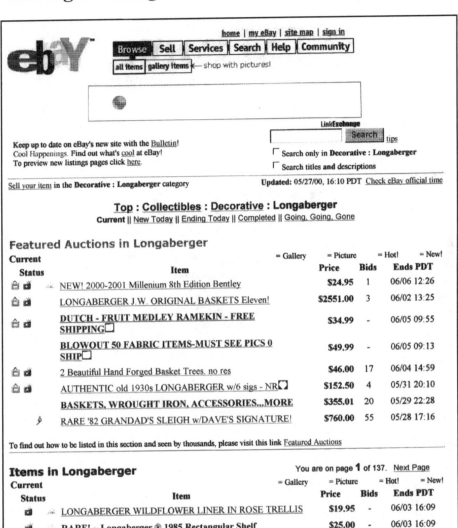

Browse | **Sell** | **Services** | **Search** | **Help** | **Community**

all items | gallery items ←—shop with pictures!

LinkExchange

Search tips

Keep up to date on eBay's new site with the Bulletin!
Cool Happenings. Find out what's cool at eBay!
To preview new listings pages click here.

☐ Search only in **Decorative : Longaberger**
☐ Search titles and descriptions

Sell your item in the **Decorative : Longaberger** category

Updated: 05/27/00, 16:10 PDT Check eBay official time

Top : Collectibles : Decorative : Longaberger

Current || New Today || Ending Today || Completed || Going, Going, Gone

Featured Auctions in Longaberger

Current   = Gallery = Picture = Hot! = New!

Status	Item	Price	Bids	Ends PDT
	NEW! 2000-2001 Millenium 8th Edition Bentley	$24.95	1	06/06 12:26
	LONGABERGER J.W. ORIGINAL BASKETS Eleven!	$2551.00	3	06/02 13:25
	DUTCH - FRUIT MEDLEY RAMEKIN - FREE SHIPPING☐	$34.99	-	06/05 09:55
	BLOWOUT 50 FABRIC ITEMS-MUST SEE PICS 0 SHIP☐	$49.99	-	06/05 09:13
	2 Beautiful Hand Forged Basket Trees. no res	$46.00	17	06/04 14:59
	AUTHENTIC old 1930s LONGABERGER w/6 sigs - NR☐	$152.50	4	05/31 20:10
	BASKETS, WROUGHT IRON, ACCESSORIES...MORE	$355.01	20	05/29 22:28
	RARE '82 GRANDAD'S SLEIGH w/DAVE'S SIGNATURE!	$760.00	55	05/28 17:16

To find out how to be listed in this section and seen by thousands, please visit this link Featured Auctions

Items in Longaberger

You are on page **1** of 137. Next Page

Current   = Gallery = Picture = Hot! = New!

Status	Item	Price	Bids	Ends PDT
	LONGABERGER WILDFLOWER LINER IN ROSE TRELLIS	$19.95	-	06/03 16:09
	RARE! ~ Longaberger ® 1985 Rectangular Shelf	$25.00	-	06/03 16:09
	Longaberger 1999 Collectors Club Ornament	$20.00	-	06/01 16:06

Search Listings

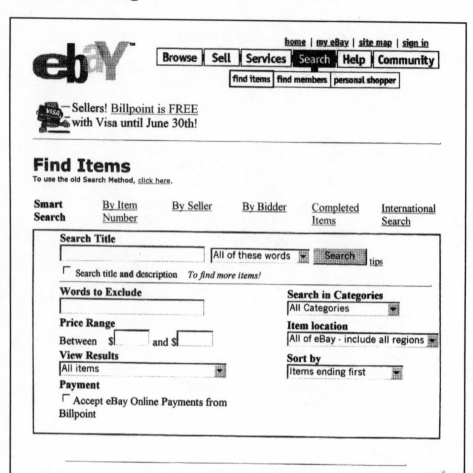

Find Items

To use the old Search Method, click here.

Smart Search	By Item Number	By Seller	By Bidder	Completed Items	International Search

Search Title

All of these words ▼ [Search] tips

☐ Search title **and** description *To find more items!*

Words to Exclude

Search in Categories
All Categories ▼

Price Range

Between $[ ] and $[ ]

Item location
All of eBay - include all regions ▼

View Results
All items ▼

Sort by
Items ending first ▼

Payment

☐ Accept eBay Online Payments from Billpoint

Announcements | Register | eBay Store | SafeHarbor (Rules & Safety) | Feedback Forum | About eBay Home | My eBay | Site Map

Browse | Sell | Services | Search | Help | Community
Find Items | Find Members | Personal Shopper

A title search, as used with online auctions, works by using keywords. Click the Search menu at the top of your screen, type in what you're looking for, and click the **Search** button. If you are looking for a specific group of words that must fall in the exact order you type them, like the Roy Rogers example above, remember to enclose the words in quotes.

You can narrow your response by navigating to a specific category and running a search from within that category. When you visit the listings page of a specific category you will see a Search box at the top right of the screen. You will also see below the search box that you have the option of running the search only within that category. This is immensely helpful when using keywords with more than one possible meaning, for instance the last name of a particular artist. If you could not narrow your search to a particular category, looking for just that name would return results from all auctions that found it. This could include sports figures on trading cards, brand names, etc.

Here's an example. I ran a search on prints by artist R. Atkinson Fox, first running a general search of the entire eBay site for just the word Fox. It returned 4192 auctions, most of which had nothing to do with R. Atkinson Fox. By going to the **Antiques & Art: Art:Fine: Prints** category first and running the search from there, specifying to search only in that category, only 157 items were returned—the vast majority of them actually being R. Atkinson Fox prints.

Bidding

Hold onto your wallet, it's time to bid! New users tend to find this addicting at first, so it's a good rule to set yourself a spending limit before you start and stick to it. Bidding at an online auction is the same as entering into a legal contract with the seller, so be prepared to go through with your purchase if you bid. Otherwise you'll find yourself with negative feedback (see Chapter 7—Advanced tips).

Once you've arrived at the description page of the item you want to bid on, either click on the bid paddle or scroll to the bottom of the page to get to the bidding section. Here you will see an electronic form where you must input the maximum amount you are willing to bid. Enter a number, without dollar signs but using a decimal in the appropriate place, and click **Review Bid**. Another screen will display where you can review the bid you are about to place and enter your eBay User ID and password. Enter them and click **Place Bid**. You're on your way.

Bidding

Browse | Sell | Services | Search | Help | Community

item view

Show me how

1955 Tin Litho Dragnet Jack Webb Target
Item #339409635

Toys, Bean Bag Plush:Vintage Tin:General

	Currently	**$9.99**	First bid	**$9.99**
Description	Quantity	**1**	# of bids	**1** (bid history) (with emails)
	Time left	**1 days, 22 hours +**	Location	**KC MO-Visit my other auctions from KC**
Bid!	Started	May-22-00 16:54:03 PDT	Country	**United States**
	Ends	May-29-00 16:54:03 PDT		✉ (mail this auction to a friend)
Watch this item	Seller (Rating)	warren*t (555) 🌟		🎁 (request a gift alert)
		(view comments in seller's Feedback Profile) (view seller's other auctions) (ask seller a question)		
	High bid	f2220@aol.com (81) 🔄		
	Payment	See item description for payment methods accepted		
		💳 Billpoint Online Payments VISA 🟦 💳 Credit Cards		
	Shipping	Seller ships internationally (worldwide). See item description for shipping charges.		

Seller assumes all responsibility for listing this item. You should contact the seller to resolve any questions before bidding. Auction currency is U.S. dollars ($) unless otherwise noted.

Description

This item is a rare 1955 Tin Litho Dragnet Jack Webb Target Shooting Gallery. It is in very good condition with no rust or dents, and just a few minor scratches. It is missing one of the plastic Jack Webb spinning targets. reads as shown in photo, with copyright 1955 Sherry TV INC. It is made to stand on it's own, or hang on wall. Does not have gun included. It measures 13" x 11". A very unique item for any collection. Buyer pays $4.65 shipping and confirmation. Thanks and Happy Bidding.

eBay™ works with a system known as Proxy Bidding, which is difficult to explain but, once understood, can be a useful tool. Proxy bidding means you may place a bid as high as you'd like but the bid amount will only advance as high as needed to surpass the previous high bidder. The higher bid you made is protected and used only if another bidder tries to surpass you. Here are some possible scenarios...

1. You've just found a 19th century quilt you like, and the current high bid is $135.00. You are willing to bid up to $225.00 for this item. You place your bid at $225.00 and are notified that you are now the high bidder and the next acceptable bid is $155.00. You scroll down to view the updated listing and see your eBay™ User ID listed as high bidder and the current high bid listed at $150.00. In this case the previous high bidder must have specified a high bid of $145.00 and when your bid of $225.00 was entered the previous high bid was surpassed only by the amount determined by eBay™ to be the bid increment for this item (in this case $5.00). If someone later bids $175.00 the high bid amount will be raised to match their bid, so you'll now be paying more for the item but you will remain the high bidder. The quilt will eventually be yours unless someone else bids more than $225.00.

2. You find the same quilt with the same current high bid of $135.00. This time when you place your bid for $225.00 you are notified that another bidder has outbid you. What has happened is that the current high bidder, when placing their bid, specified an amount higher than $225.00. You will now have to raise the amount you are willing to bid if you really want this quilt. After receiving the notice of being outbid you can click the Back button on your browser to go back to the bid section and place another bid if you'd like. Just be aware that any time you use the Back button to get to a screen where your password was entered you will have to reenter it. It is omitted for security reasons.

Be sure to read the Chapter 7—Advanced Tips about the danger of placing a high bid in the hopes nobody else will come close. Never bid more than you are willing to pay, because you just might end up paying close to your top bid.

SELLERS

There are certain fees associated with selling on eBay™ but they are quite a bit lower than your local auction house will charge and you are exposing your merchandise to a much larger audience. Of course you must store the item until it sells, and pack and ship it to the buyer. If you're willing and able to do these things, let's sell some stuff!

Establish Your Account

In previous editions of this book I have recommended that for convenience and ease of credit approval you open an account using your credit card during the registration confirmation process. It is now mandatory on eBay™ that you do so. If you previously registered as a buyer and now want to sell but cannot because you have no credit card on file, you can go to the Site Map and register your credit card by clicking **Seller Account—Place or Update My Credit Card**. Your information is taken over a secured line, and I've not heard of anyone in eBay™'s vast user base having problems with billing and/or credit information getting into the wrong hands by submitting it online. Once your card is accepted, it will be used to bill you automatically for any fees you incur each month.

List Your Item

Click the **Sell** box at the top of the eBay™ homepage. You'll come to the categories page, where you must select a broad category that fits the description of your item. Click on one, and next you'll see a page where you must enter your user ID and password, a title for your merchandise, and a form that allows you to expand the broad category you've chosen into subcategories—simply click on a subcategory and it will expand into additional subcategories that you can again click on, allowing you to place your item where collectors of that particular item look first. Next comes your description—be sure to describe the item accurately and with as much detail as possible. Next to having a photo posted, the description is the most important part of your listing. Adding photos (covered in depth in Chapter 7—Advanced Tips) is also done at this time. There are then several other options you can select, like making the title of your item bold which makes it stand out more against the others in the category. I recommend not using any of these options unless you know you really have something special for sale, as you pay extra for each one.

Establishing a Sellers Account on eBay™

 ™

home | my eBay | site map | sign in

Browse ‖ Sell ‖ Services ‖ Search ‖ Help ‖ Community

Place or update your credit card on your eBay account

Use this secure form to place your credit card on your eBay account or to update your credit card information for automatic payment of your monthly invoice. The transmitted credit card information is protected by the industry standard *SSL*.

- Beginning October 22, 1999, all new sellers must provide a valid credit card. (why is this required?)
- Your credit card information will be placed on your eBay account within 24 hours of receipt.
- When you place your credit card on eBay for the **first time**, eBay will attempt to authorize your card. The response from your credit card company will appear on your account status page as either approved or declined. If approved, eBay will bill your credit card each month for your previous month's fees.
- If you already have a credit card on file with us, you can change or update your credit card information at anytime.
- Your credit card will normally be charged 7 to 10 days after receipt of your invoice for the previous month's invoice amount.

Click here for more information about eBay Platinum VISA.

 STEP 1
Enter your eBay User ID or email address.

User ID or Email Address	

 STEP 2
Enter your eBay password.

Password	
	(forgotten it?)

STEP 3
Enter your name exactly as it appears on your credit card.

Your Name	

Establishing a Sellers Account on eBay™

STEP 4

Enter your billing address exactly as it appears on your credit card statement. **Your billing address is defined as the address where you receive your credit card bill. This normally is your home address.** If the address that you have entered does not match the address on your credit card statement, your verification will be denied.

	_____
	Street
Credit Card Billing Address **(The address where you receive your credit card bill.)**	_____
	City
	_____
	State/Province
	_____
	Zip Code
	United States ▼
	Country

STEP 5

Enter your credit card number.

Credit Card Number	_____ Visa, MasterCard, American Express or Discover
	e.g., 4123-4567-8910-1234 eBay Welcomes **VISA**

STEP 6

Enter the expiration date of your credit card.

Expiration Date	**Month**: `--` ▼ Day: `--` ▼ **Year**: `----` ▼
	Leave day as --, if day on credit card is not listed

STEP 7

Click "Submit" to place your credit card information on your eBay account. When you place your credit card on eBay for the **first time**, eBay will attempt to authorize your card. The response from your credit card company will appear on your account status page as either approved or declined. If approved, eBay will bill your credit card each month for your previous month's fees.

Click	Submit

Click here to review your account status .

List Your Item

home | my eBay | site map | sign in

Browse | **Sell** | **Services** | **Search** | **Help** | **Community**

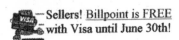

sell your item form

Sellers! Billpoint is FREE with Visa until June 30th!

[Search] Smart Search

☐ Search titles **and** descriptions

Sell Your Item

Related Links: • New to Selling? • Seller Tips • Fees • Registration
• Free Shipping Estimates from iShip.com

Before you can sell...

1) You must be a registered eBay user.
2) You must provide a valid credit card if you are new to selling. Why?
3) Make sure your item is allowed on eBay.

First, choose a Main Category:
(you'll choose a subcategory on the next page)

Why did this page change?

You can still choose from all the categories at once by clicking here.

Antiques & Art
Fine art, glass, ceramics, furniture, and more.

Automotive--eBay Motors
Used cars, collector cars, motorcycles, and related parts and accessories.

Books, Movies, Music
Magazines, entertainment memorabilia, and musical instruments

Coins and Stamps
Currency, exonumia, and scripophily

Photo & Electronics
Audio, electronics, and photo and video equipment

Collectibles
Everything from advertising to comic books to writing instruments

Computers
Hardware, software, games, domain names, and services

Dolls, Doll Houses
Antique, collectible, contemporary, miniatures, and furniture

Jewelry, Gemstones
Antique, comtemporary, watches, artist, and beads

Pottery & Glass
China, porcelain, and stoneware

Sports
Autographs, memorabilia, trading cards, equipment, and recreation

Toys, Bean Bag Plush
Action figures, games, hobbies, and vintage

Everything Else
Clothing, household, equipment, tools, tickets, real estate and more

List Your Item

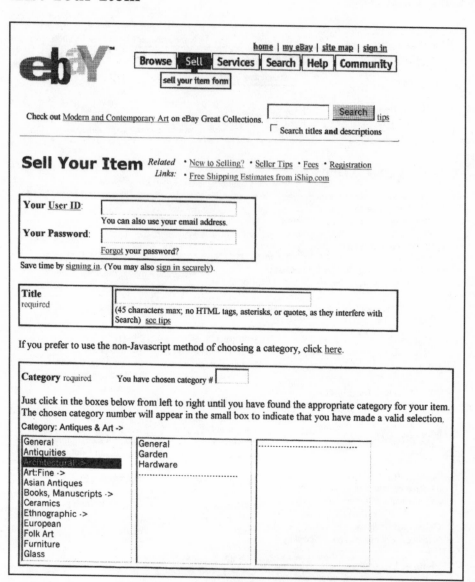

List Your Item

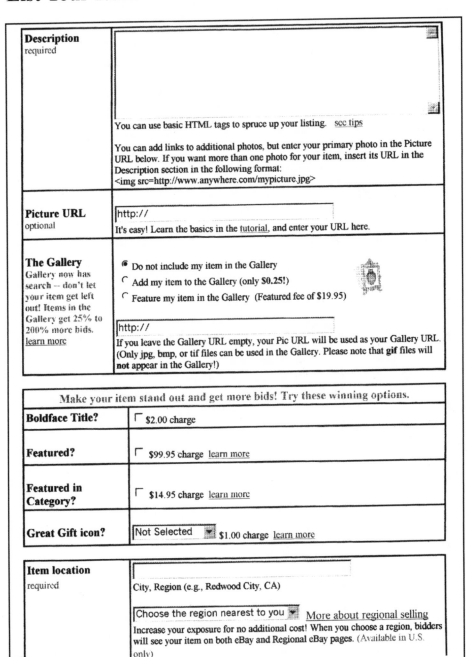

Description required	*(large text entry box)* You can use basic HTML tags to spruce up your listing. see tips You can add links to additional photos, but enter your primary photo in the Picture URL below. If you want more than one photo for your item, insert its URL in the Description section in the following format: <img src=http://www.anywhere.com/mypicture.jpg>
Picture URL optional	http:// It's easy! Learn the basics in the tutorial, and enter your URL here.
The Gallery Gallery now has search -- don't let your item get left out! Items in the Gallery get 25% to 200% more bids. learn more	⦿ Do not include my item in the Gallery ○ Add my item to the Gallery (only $0.25!) ○ Feature my item in the Gallery (Featured fee of $19.95) http:// If you leave the Gallery URL empty, your Pic URL will be used as your Gallery URL. (Only jpg, bmp, or tif files can be used in the Gallery. Please note that **gif** files will **not** appear in the Gallery!)

Make your item stand out and get more bids! Try these winning options.	
Boldface Title?	☐ $2.00 charge
Featured?	☐ $99.95 charge learn more
Featured in Category?	☐ $14.95 charge learn more
Great Gift icon?	Not Selected ▼ $1.00 charge learn more

Item location required	*(text entry box)* City, Region (e.g., Redwood City, CA) Choose the region nearest to you ▼ More about regional selling Increase your exposure for no additional cost! When you choose a region, bidders will see your item on both eBay and Regional eBay pages. (Available in U.S. only)

List Your Item

	United States ▼ Country

Payment Methods Choose all that you will accept	☐ Money Order/Cashiers Check ☐ Personal Check ☐ Visa/MasterCard ☐ COD (cash on delivery) ☐ Discover ☐ American Express ☑ See Item Description ☐ Other
Billpoint online payments VISA ▭ ▭	☐ Billpoint online payments. learn more Accept Visa, MasterCard, or Discover from your winning bidders online. All Visa orders are free with Billpoint. If you are not a registered Billpoint seller, apply now. Click this icon to find out how to add it to your item Description: [SECURE ONLINE / BILLPOINT] Billpoint supports international orders from these countries.
Escrow	◯ I will accept escrow, buyer pays (recommended) ◯ I will pay escrow ⦿ I will not accept escrow, (if selected, the Escrow section will not appear on the item listing) learn more

Where will you ship?	⦿ Will ship to United States only
	 ◯ Will ship internationally (worldwide)
	 ◯ Will ship to United States and the following regions: (Check all that apply)
	
	      ☐ Canada
	      ☐ Europe
	      ☐ Australasia
	      ☐ Asia
	      ☐ South America
	      ☐ Africa
	      ☐ Mexico and Central America
	      ☐ Middle East
	      ☐ Caribbean
	
	 see tips

Who pays for shipping?	☐ Seller Pays Shipping ☐ Buyer Pays Fixed Amount ☐ Buyer Pays Actual Shipping Cost ☑ See Item Description

List Your Item

Quantity required	1 If quantity is more than one, then you will have a Dutch Auction (Multiple Item Auction). see tips
Minimum bid (in $) required	_____ per item see tips (e.g., 2.00 -- Please do not include commas or currency symbols, such as $.)
Duration required	7 ▼ days

Reserve Price (in $) optional	Enter reserve price (optional): _____ see tips (e.g., 15.00 -- Please do not include commas or currency symbols, such as $.) Careful! Reserve Auction fees will apply if your item does not sell (learn more).
Private Auction? optional	☐ Please don't use this unless you have a specific reason. learn more

☐ Remember my selling preferences. (sections marked with   )

Press the "review" button below to see what fees are due immediately and what fees may be due if your item sells. You will not incur any fees until you accept the terms disclosed in the next screen.

Press review to review and place your listing.

Press clear form to clear the form and start over.

Note: If the Back button on your browser erases your information on this form, find out how to fix this.

Top Questions From This Page
• How do I add a picture to my listing?   • How do I set up a seller account? • Are there fees when I sell something?   • Can I list this type of item? • How do I pay eBay for fees?   • Why isn't my picture showing up? • How can I change something or cancel my   • How do I add extra pictures after I've listed listing completely?   my item?

Next, specify your item location. This is useful particularly if you are selling large merchandise like furniture. Bidders in your local area might be willing to bid higher if they know they can pick up large pieces and not have to pay shipping. You'll also have to check boxes for the payment options you will accept, if you will accept escrow, what countries you will ship to, and who pays for shipping. You then list the quantity of items (or groups of items) available in this auction—for instance if you are selling three glass coasters together it is considered one item. Selling them separately would qualify your auction as a *Dutch auction,* which means you have more than one identical item you are selling individually. Next the minimum bid you will accept is entered, and the duration (3, 5, 7, or 10 days) is specified. If you have a price in mind and won't take less, enter this price as the *reserve*. Reserve protects you in case the bidding is low; you don't have to sell your item unless your reserve price is met.

When you have filled in and/or selected all of the necessary items, Click **Review** to see a synopsis of the information you've input and a facsimile of your listing. If everything checks out click **Submit My Listing**. A confirmation number will be displayed in your browser window that you should record for future reference, and your item is listed!

Keeping Track of Your eBay™ Transactions

The easiest and best way to track your activity on eBay™ is to take advantage of a very useful page called simply My eBay™. Each unique registered user has their own My eBay™ page—you can access yours from the **Site Map** link. From here you can monitor every active listing you have posted and the current high bid on it, every item that you have bid on and the current high bid, and the last three feedback transactions someone has posted about you. You can even specify four categories (your favorites) that you can instantly link to from the page. It is a well-designed and extremely helpful addition to the eBay™ community.

After the Sale

Shortly after the auction ends, you will receive an automatic e-mail message telling you the auction is over, how much the high bid was, and the e-mail address of the high bidder. Have your items packaged and weighed because you will now have to contact the high bidder and inform them of the shipping cost. A small home postage scale is helpful here, but expect to make occasional trips to the post office for accurate costs on larger packages. For help in determining shipping costs for the U.S. Postal Service, refer to Appendix B of this book. You can also get help online at the following Web sites…

U.S. Post Office	**www.usps.gov**
Federal Express	**www.fedex.com**
UPS	**www.ups.com**

Establish policies concerning insurance (I recommend offering it and letting the high bidder decide) and if you will assess a handling charge. You have three days to contact the high bidder with this information and give them a final price (including shipping, insurance, and handling) for the item. Specify payment terms—can you accept credit cards? If so, supply the high bidder with your phone number so that they may contact you with their card number if they wish. Most sellers accept personal checks with the condition that the merchandise will be held for a short period of time to allow the check to clear; however some sellers will ship immediately to buyers with high feedback ratings. If the buyer sends you a money order, treat it as cash and ship the merchandise within 24—48 hours.

Silver spoons with figural handles.

One of a set of ice cream dishes copyrighted in 1900 and made in France for the Richard Briggs Co. of Boston.

An urn-shaped silver teapot with molded heads and chased leaf decorations made by Meriden Company in the 1870s.

CHAPTER 6
COLLECTOR'S TOOL BOX

Internet sites that specialize in providing tools for users of online auctions have become big business. Help is available for anything from adding counters to your listings to managing your inventory. Many of these tools are available at no charge, and there is also a small but increasing number of sites that have started to charge fees to help sellers who routinely list hundreds of items weekly do so more efficiently. If you are considering going into selling online at auctions as a full time profession, be advised that the amount of time it takes to manage hundreds of items is the #1 reason more people don't do it successfully.

The part of the online auction process that more people find difficult than any other is learning to use *FTP* (file transfer protocol) to get their photos uploaded to a server where potential bidders can access them. Guess what! You don't have to learn FTP or even have the software loaded on your computer!

A very useful tool available to collectors with Internet access is AuctionWatch.com (*http://www.auctionwatch.com*). One of the many features of the AuctionWatch.com site is that they provide, free of charge, space on their server to each member (registration is also free) and an automatic upload feature that makes this process unbelievably easy.

Here's how it works. Go to the AuctionWatch.com site and click on the **Auction Manager** link. You'll be taken to the Auction Manager login page where you can enter if you're a registered member or, if not, register. The only required information to register on AuctionWatch.com is your name, address and e-mail address. Other than that, you must pick a screen name and password just as you have to do to register with any online auction. As always, remember your password or you won't be able to access the features of the site.

Once your registration is confirmed, you can begin using the free image hosting feature. Return to the Auction Manager login page and enter your username and password. You'll arrive at the Control Panel where your current activity and options are displayed. Click on **Image Hosting** and you'll come to a page from where you can browse your computer's hard drive contents for the photos you want to upload. Click

http://www.auctionwatch.com

a browse button and a **Choose File** window will open, allowing you to navigate through your computer until you find the photo you need. Select the correct photo, click **Open**, and the file name will appear in the upload window of the page.

You can upload three photos at a time, and each must be less than 350K in size. This is quite generous, and I don't recommend you run photos of that size on online auctions anyway—they simply take too long to load. Prospective bidders will tire of waiting and leave your auction, costing you bids and higher prices. Your goal should be keeping your files to 60K or less. Once you have one, two, or three files displayed in the upload windows, simply click the **Upload** button. Your files will be transmitted and stored on the AuctionWatch.com server, you will get a message telling you the upload was successful, and the photo(s) will display.

http://www.auctionworks.com

The next step is to select the photo(s) you want to use in your auction. Simply click on the empty box under the photo(s) you want to use. Next, click on the **Attach to Existing** button and you will see some code that you simply copy and paste into the item description box of the auction you are starting. Believe me, it's even easier than it sounds!

One more thing you should be aware of when you use any public site like this—as more people begin to use it, server access typically slows down and your photo may load a bit slower for potential bidders than if you were using your ISP's server. However, if you follow the strategies outlined in my companion book *The ABCs of Making Money Online* and keep your photos to a minimum size, you will get acceptable performance from AuctionWatch.com. Or if you prefer to FTP files to your ISP's server, learn how in Chapter 7 of this book.

New sites are springing up to offer free photo posting services and other tools, one of which is Auction Works *(http://www.auctionworks.com)*. Auction Works, previously an online auction, has converted to an online tools site and offers a free e-commerce enabled storefront, free image hosting, and inventory management. A collector's resource section was not yet open when this book went to press, but you may want to check and see what develops there.

http://www.auctions.goto.com

Home | Web Search | Shopping | Auctions

GoTo.com Auctions made simple. uBid.com **Up to 70% OFF**

Welcome | Search | Bid | Sell | Learn | Community

Log In | Help

SEARCH ALL AUCTIONS [ ] FETCH

Member Login:

User ID [ ] Password [ ]

[LOG IN]

Become a member!
Forgot your password?
Why Join?

Bid.
Track auctions and trends with Bidder Services.

Sell.
Sell more in less time with AuctionManager.™

Learn.
Choose a topic and learn all about online auctions.

Browse Categories

Antiques
Antiques (post-1900), Antiques (pre-1900), Furniture, ...

Collectibles
Trading Cards, Collector Plates, Comic Books, ...

Dolls & Figures
Barbie, Dolls, Figures, ...

Jewelry & Gemstones
Jewelry, Men's, Gemstones, ...

Photo & Electronics
Consumer Electronics, Photo Equipment, Radio Equipment, ...

Sports Memorabilia
Trading Cards, Baseball, Singles, ...

Travel & Real Estate NEW
Vacation Packages, Hotels & Accomodations, Cruises, ...

Coins & Stamps
Coins, US, Stamps, ...

Computers & Internet
Domain Names, Hardware, PC Systems, ...

Entertainment NEW
Music, Books, Movies, ...

Miscellaneous
Art: Nude, Weird Stuff, Clothing, ...

Pottery & Glass
Glass, Pottery, Depression, ...

Toys & Bean Bag Plush
Transformers, Fisher Price, Ty Retired Beanies. ...

Vehicles NEW
SUVs & Trucks, General Cars, Automobiles, ...

Sellers -

ebY

Join our Affiliate Program EARN MONEY!

GREAT JOBS AHEAD CLICK HERE

About GoTo Auctions

New Seller Features

Our enhanced tools include invoicing and personalized storefronts. Check out our new AuctionManager™ features and sell more today!

GoTo Auctions Launches B2B Auction Search

Search over 30 business exchanges on B2BRover.

http://www.honesty.com

AuctionRover.com *(http://www.auctionrover.com)* features both an online auction as well as auction tools. They offer both bidder and seller services, including a feature called price trending. Price trending tracks sales from a large cross-section of online sources and compiles the data into charts and tables that you can use to get a good idea of what particular items are selling for. This is a particularly useful feature for items that are commonly traded online, such as coins, stamps, and computers.

When you use your own ISP to host your auction photos but still want a counter keeping track of your page *hits,* point your browser to *http://www.honesty.com.* Here you can register and easily attach a counter to your eBay™, Amazon.com, or other auction—even your personal home page! The counters come in a wide variety of styles, and there is a statistical chart you can view on each counter that shows you what days and times your counter is registering the most visitors. All of this service is absolutely free—paid for by the advertising you will see on the site.

I have asked many people what they use counters for—what type of information they glean from using one. The most common answer is, in the case of online auctions, that it helps them identify what items are hot and which ones are not. I personally would rather gauge how "hot" an item is from the number of bids it receives and the final auction value, but nonetheless this seems to be a valid reason for some to have a counter on their auction pages. If you're a statistics buff and believe that numbers don't lie, the statistical data now being offered by Honesty.com may allow you to identify peak bidding times and therefore give you an indicator of the best times to start and end your auctions.

Honesty.com has evolved from humble beginnings to offer more and better services every few months, and I'm sure they will continue in that vein. Tuck this site away in your favorites folder and visit regularly to keep up with the coming auction tools they will be sure to offer in the near future.

A free counter site already offering some other Web tools is *http://www.beseen.com.* Although the auction counters must be cut and pasted into your auction listing, whereas with Honesty.com it is automatic for eBay™ and Amazon.com auctions, here you can build your own home page and add a personalized search engine to your site. You can add a feature to your Web site to survey your site visitors, and is a way to more easily navigate your site. All of this is free for the asking, just by joining Beseen.com.

http://www.beseen.com

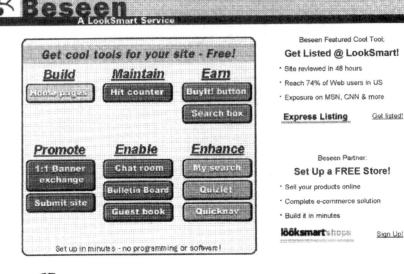

Get cool tools for your site - Free!

Build
- Home pages

Maintain
- Hit counter

Earn
- BuyIt! button
- Search box

Promote
- 1:1 Banner exchange
- Submit site

Enable
- Chat room
- Bulletin Board
- Guest book

Enhance
- My search
- Quizlet
- Quicknav

Set up in minutes - no programming or software!

Beseen Featured Cool Tool:

Get Listed @ LookSmart!

- Site reviewed in 48 hours
- Reach 74% of Web users in US
- Exposure on MSN, CNN & more

Express Listing   Get listed!

Beseen Partner:

Set Up a FREE Store!

- Sell your products online
- Complete e-commerce solution
- Build it in minutes

looksmart shops   Sign Up!

Get talking in the **CHAT ZONE**

Link to LookSmart's Beseen!

Home | Help | Advertising | Contact Us | Edit Chat Room | The Chat Zone | Web Graphics | LookSmart

http://tsinc.simplenet.com/index.hts

Welcome to Trouble Shooters Inc, the home of free PC support. You can ask the volunteer support staff in the Ask Us Tower for assistance with any problem you are having. We recommend you walk over to the Solutions Library Tower before you ask your question.

TSInc is always looking for new volunteers who have a working knowledge of Windows Software, Operating Systems, or Hardware. This is a learning experience as well as a help desk. So visit the Volunteer Control Tower and see what is in store for you.

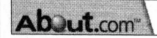 Your Email Address.
Join our TSInc New Features mailing list. This will tell you about any new features which are added to the site, and that you should know about.

[Join]
[Delete]

PC Troubleshooting

Yes, if you know where to look, you can even find free help in troubleshooting your PC problems. A group of volunteers who try, and usually succeed, in helping you through computer related problems can be found at *http://tsinc.simplenet.com/index.hts*. Here you can search a database of previous problems and their solutions, and if you don't find your particular problem you can ask for help. The help form will ask some simple questions such as your computer experience level and give you the opportunity to explain your problem. In some cases you will receive more than one reply, giving you several options to try. When you find one that works, you should report back how the problem was fixed so that it can be added to the database.

Finding Your Way

As I've told you, the Internet is much more than auction sites and malls. If you've ever heard the expression "if you can dream it, you can do it" the Internet proves that in many cases that statement is true. You can even find directions to that big auction you want to attend in a town several hours away with the click of a mouse.

Mapquest (*http://www.mapquest.com*) gives you the ability to type in the names of two different towns and not only get driving directions between the two, but total miles and the estimated drive time. Directions are supplied in either map form, or a "printer-friendly" format that you can print out and take with you. The site also offers a travel guide, travel deals, and a local city guide.

American Automobile Association (*http://www.aaa.com*) also offers driving directions online, but you must be a member to access them. If you are an AAA member you can also order a TripTik® or maps online and have them delivered to your home.

http://www.mapquest.com

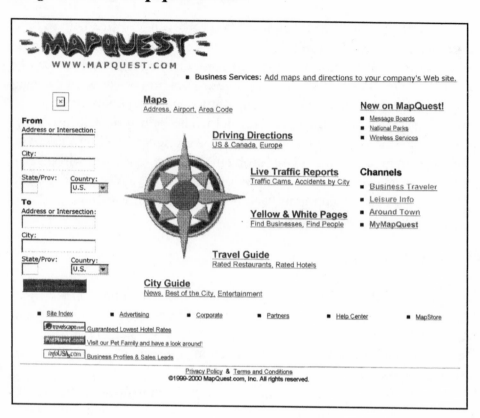

Pack and Ship

I'm partial to the United States Postal Service. They offer dependable service at reasonable prices and throw in free supplies to boot! If you haven't taken advantage of their online services, visit *http://www.usps.gov* and get with the program! While they can't weigh your package for you (at least at the Web site they can't—visit your local post office and they'll be happy to), they do supply a rate calculator that will give you an accurate shipping cost for anything from priority mail to parcel post to oversized packages. You can track express mail, and confirm delivery for priority mail and parcel post. There is also a zip code locator that identifies zip codes with towns, and another tool that gives you the zip+4 code for any address.

Oh, I mentioned free supplies, didn't I? By visiting *http://supplies.usps.gov* you can take advantage of free boxes, tape, labels, and other goodies that will make it much easier to fulfill your shipping responsibilities. While most local post office branches carry a selection of the more commonly used boxes, the Web site will give you a list of many other available materials.

There is now a tool on eBay™ that allows potential bidders to calculate their shipping costs without even contacting you! Through iShip.com, you can add a link to your auction listings that will allow prospective bidders to calculate shipping costs from your zip code to theirs. The process happens when you are listing your item, and can be accessed from a link on the eBay™ Sell Your Item page.

Clicking on the link brings you to a form where you input the following information: 1) Select the carriers you are willing to use. The choices are the United States Postal Service, Federal Express, United Parcel Service, and Airborne Express. 2) Select your pickup/drop off option. You can choose from taking the package to a drop box, taking it to a branch office of your carrier, having a scheduled pickup at your location or calling for an immediate pickup at your location. 3) Enter the zip code from where the package will be shipped. 4) Enter the weight of the package. You must also supply dimensions if the package is oversized. 5) Specify the amount of insurance on the package, if any. 6) Specify the amount of handling charges you wish to add, if any. You can specify handling charges as a percentage of the shipping charges or a fixed amount. You then preview what the bidder will see, and you can even plug in a zip code and have it calculate shipping charges on the information you have just entered if you want to double check the amounts being displayed to bidders. You then click on a button that creates the HTML for your link, which you then copy and paste into your item description.

When a buyer clicks on the link in your description, they need only specify their zip code, whether they are a business or a residence, and if they need a guaranteed delivery time. A chart is then displayed showing the shipping amount for this particular package, with a breakdown by the different carriers the seller has specified. This effectively solves a problem that has plagued buyers since the inception of online auctions—wondering what shipping will cost. While it adds an extra minute or two to the listing process, the value added is enormous and I expect this type of information to someday become an important part of the auction process.

eBay a-go-go™

If you've really become an eBay™ junkie and can't wait to find out when you've been outbid on an item, win an auction, or sell something, SkyTel has the program for you. eBay a-go-go™ notifies you via wireless pager when any of these three events occurs, as well as provides a regular dose of eBay™ news.

Along with a one-time $20 activation charge, for $55 you purchase 2000 message units and receive a unique eBay™ pager. Each auction notification, on average, expends four of those message units, which means your initial purchase nets you roughly 500 auction notifications. The notification itself is a condensed version of the message you receive via your computer e-mail, and you continue to receive those messages on your computer. There are no contracts to sign and everything is paid up front, but the message units must be used within six months of the time you receive your pager. Additional message units can then be purchased on a sliding scale cost.

This unit also functions as a regular pager that friends, family, and business associates can use to contact you. For complete details on this program as well as available add-on options like voice mail and caller ID, go to *http://www.skytel.com/ebay.*

If you have a current wireless device that has an e-mail address and accepts alphanumeric messaging, you can sign up for the basic service and use your existing device, however you will not receive the eBay™ news broadcasts or be able to access your messages via telephone as you can with the SkyTel service.

Site Maps

Let's not forget about the auction sites themselves, and the wealth of online help they make available. The easiest way to get an overview of what is available on any major auction is to visit their *site map* (some refer to it as a *site guide*). A site map is simply a page that lists a brief explanation of all of the options available to the visitor as well as links to get to any part of the site easily. eBay™ provides a help section on their site map, with links to bulletin boards where users can ask for assistance, guides for both buyers and sellers, direct support for new users, even an images/HTML board for assistance in those areas. The boards are part of what make eBay™ a community—many users monitor the boards and offer useful advice to others seeking assistance.

The souvenir book, *The Rocky Mountains of Colorado,* contains colored engravings and has a 1913 copyright date.

Statehood quarters from the 1999 and 2000 issues, along with silver dollars, and other "collectible" coins.

A Victorian oil painting of an exotically costumed "Egyptian" lady.

Chapter 7
Advanced Tips for
Online Auction Users

Bidding

So you've tried bidding before reading this chapter? You're probably already acquainted with an online auction fact of life—wanting to be the winning bidder of a particular auction often means you must be at your computer during the last 5—10 minutes watching the bid progress. Many experienced auction goers wait until the last few minutes to bid. During the last two minutes of the auction they often win the item you've been high bidder on for the past six days. This type of bidding is called *sniping* and the people who practice it are referred to as *snipers*.

One remedy to this would be placing a bid so high that nobody else would consider matching it. You might get the item, but often pay more than necessary due to a phenomenon known as *auction frenzy*. Auction frenzy is when several bidders begin to compete in the last few minutes of the auction and throw common sense to the wind—owning the item becomes paramount regardless of price. If you're the unlucky person sitting in the high bidder spot, having bid a foolishly high amount to protect yourself, you may wind up paying a lot more than you bargained for.

If you can't be at your computer when an auction ends for an item you *must* have, place a bid as high as you are willing to go and hope for the best. If you don't get the item don't despair—quite often another identical or similar and perhaps even better item will come along eventually. Keep watching and use the title search option to locate another example of your must-have item. I've seen three separate items almost identical to each other listed over three consecutive weeks (one week each) by three different sellers on eBay™, each described as rare. Had I wanted to, I could have owned three of the same "rare" items within a time span of 21 days. Just hang on—you'll find another item to take the place of the one you lost.

Sniping

While we're on the subject of sniping, here's how it's done. When you find an auction item you really want to own, bookmark it and make a note of when the auction is closing. Fifteen minutes before that closing, sit down at your computer, log onto the Internet, find the auction, and get ready to bid the maximum amount you are willing to go. Enter everything just as if you are going to place the bid, but do not click the **Place Bid** bar.

Now launch a new browser window. Simply double-click on the browser icon or do whatever it is you do to open your Internet Explorer, Netscape, or other browser software. A new window will open over top of the one you were just preparing to place your bid in. Adjust the sizes of the windows so that you can view both of them at the same time. This is accomplished in Internet Explorer by placing the cursor over the lower right corner of the window until it turns into a double-headed arrow. You can then click and drag the corner of the windows until they are the size you want them to be.

In the second window you opened, navigate to the auction listing again. Now you have one window showing you the current bid price and time left in the auction and another with the **Place Bid** bar showing. Repeatedly click **Refresh** on the window that shows you the time remaining, clicking at time intervals you are comfortable with, until the clock winds down to less than one minute. Now click on the other window to activate it and immediately click the **Place Bid** bar. Your maximum bid will be recorded.

The potential problem with this method is that if your maximum bid is not high enough to surpass the proxy bid entered by the current high bidder, you won't have enough time left to place another bid if you wanted to. This is why you should just go ahead and place a bid for the maximum amount you are willing to pay—don't try to "nickel and dime" your way into the high bid position.

Of course, there are times when you just can't be at your computer when an auction ends. For instances like this, I recommend you purchase software called *Merlin,* available for $12.95 from Jason Novak. Merlin has an automatic snipe program that will place bids for you while you're away, as well as other tools that make it more convenient to manage your online auction activities. You can find out more about the capabilities of this extremely useful software in my companion book, *The ABCs of Making Money Online.* Order this software by visiting *http://www.pctechzone.com.*

Selling

There are times when it is advantageous to have your item listed in more than one category. Unfortunately, eBay™ does not allow you to do this. There is a way to duplicate your listing in different categories on eBay™ too, with some extra time and expense, and if you have a desirable item that should be exposed to more than one type of collector I recommend you invest the time and money to do it.

First, submit your listing in the category where you think it fits best, or will be exposed to the most interested bidders. Once the listing is confirmed, visit the auction page and copy the URL of the auction by highlighting it in the browser address window and clicking on **Copy** under your **Edit** menu. You now have a copy of the address of your auction on your computer *clipboard,* and you can duplicate it by selecting **Paste**, again under the **Edit** menu.

Now return to the Sell Your Item page. Use the same title as you did for your "main" auction, but select a different category this time. When you are doing your description, instead of describing the item you will simply type the following...

<BLOCKQUOTE>This listing is not active. Please do not place your bid for this item here, as it will not be recognized as a valid bid. If you want to bid on this item, click <A href="Paste">here</A></BLOCKQUOTE>

Substitute the address you copied to your clipboard for the word **Paste** in the example above, and enclose that address in quotes. Also be sure to use the opening and closing angle brackets just as you see them in the example. Without even trying hard, you've just created an HTML *anchor* tag.

What you are doing is creating a *link* from this page to the actual listing. When the bidder clicks on the word "here" they will be whisked to the auction where bids are being accepted. Now all you have to do is finish filling out any remaining information and submitting the auction. You will end up with two auctions for the same item, one linked to the other. Post a photo in both auctions to pique bidder interest so they are more inclined to click your link to get to the "real" auction.

Of course, you will pay for the second listing. If you start the bidding below $10.00 with no reserve, you will only pay $0.25 extra. You will also pay the regular eBay™ commission on the high bid achieved by those bidders who will invariably not understand what is going on and place a bid on the "wrong" auction. There are potential pitfalls with this method, and if you are uncomfortable doing it for any reason, don't. It does work, and if you monitor your auctions and e-mail bidders right away who place bids on the wrong auction to explain what you are doing, misunderstandings can be avoided.

Leave Feedback

You should leave feedback after every transaction, whether you were the buyer or the seller. Feedback helps identify the auction users you should avoid buying from and possibly selling to. Some sellers post in their descriptions that they reserve the right to refuse to sell to users with negative feedback. So it goes without saying you should do everything in your power to keep negatives out of your feedback stable.

Don't be afraid to leave negative feedback for someone who deserves it, but by all means try to settle the situation amicably first. Allow adequate time for the offending party to make good on their promise and e-mail them with non-threatening words of encouragement occasionally. If you've gotten no response for over two weeks, it's time to consider lodging a public complaint via the feedback system. Many people won't do this for fear of retaliation in the form of the offending party leaving negative feedback for them also. Do your duty! Most experienced users understand that one or two negatives surrounded by many more positives means you've been accused unfairly and will give you the benefit of the doubt.

Post a Photo

Using a photo is a must for both buyer and seller, and the photo should be clear and sharp as well as small in file size (50K or less is best). Buyers stay clear of listings without photos because not only can't they pick up the object and examine it, they can't even see it. Even the best description can't always do justice to an object, and a potential buyer doesn't know for sure that the item exists if you haven't displayed a photo of it. Conversely, sellers will realize higher bids for items with photos as opposed to the same item without one. To get a photo posted on the Internet you must have a means of getting the photo into digital form (i.e., digital camera or scanner), an Internet Service Provider that provides some storage capacity on their server (see Chapter 3—Choosing an Internet Service Provider), and software known as *FTP* (file transfer protocol). It's not nearly as daunting as it sounds—let's look closer.

If you will be listing items on a limited basis, begin by asking your friends if they know anyone who has a color photo scanner. You might be surprised at how many computer users have them in their living rooms and are willing to do some scans for you at a reasonable cost. Your local office supply store may be able to direct you to someone who can do scans on an as-needed basis. But if you plan to do any amount of volume selling, or just plan to be in the online auction game for the long haul, getting your own equipment to post photos on the Internet is a must.

Scanners that can handle color photos, at least at first glance, are the least expensive way to start. Visit any computer superstore or Web site and you'll find color scanners for less than $100.00. You may want to consider some things before running out and buying one, though. First, it will take practice and patience to learn to use the scanner. While it may not be difficult for the computer-savvy, it's just not as easy as the point-and-click ease of a digital camera. Scanners are also notorious for not interfacing with your computer easily; some require you to get inside the computer case and add new hardware. And while a few of the things you want to scan can be laid directly on the scanner bed, others have to be photographed first anyway due to size, weight, and other considerations. When you photograph with film you have to buy a roll, use the entire roll, take it to be developed, wait for it to be developed, and then scan the photographs. It is neither time nor cost efficient.

If you decide to go the scanner route, most of the flatbed scanners on the market today are adequate for purposes of reproducing a photo of your merchandise. Look for a scanner rated at least 36-bit. The higher the bit rating, the better dynamic range the scanner has, meaning it will pick out detail, especially shadow detail, better. Of course with the better dynamic ranges come higher prices. You can get a clear, sharp photo with a 24-bit scanner, but for the slight difference in price go for the higher bit ratings.

Digital cameras have dropped in price drastically since their introduction just a few short years ago. You can now buy a low-end digital camera, which is suitable for most online auction merchandise, at prices not much higher than the 36-bit scanners. It may not pick up the pattern in your depression glass as well as you'd like, and if you can afford the high-end digital camera for your auction listings you should purchase one. But don't let cost get in the way of having a way of taking digital photos—if you can't afford the best camera buy a low-end one. Many bidders have an extensive library of books that contain photos of the items they are interested in, and these books can show the detail your camera missed.

With the digital camera you simply take the photos and download them via a cable connected from the camera to your computer. Sony makes a very popular camera (*Mavica*) that stores the photos on a floppy disk that you simply remove from the camera and slide into the floppy drive of your computer. No film to buy. No developing costs. You can take one photo or several. And if you don't like a photo once you see it, you can redo it in minutes. Once you try a digital camera you'll find a lot of alternative uses for it, like e-mailing Sis some photos of your new doll you bought on eBay™.

Whether you decide to go with the scanner or the camera, be sure your purchase includes cables and software to transfer the image from the device to your computer. Some basic image editing software is also necessary that will allow you to brighten dark photos, control the color saturation, and *crop* the photo to its minimal size. Always crop the photo as small as possible to cut out the background or unimportant elements. The smaller the photo the faster it will load to the browser of a potential bidder.

You must also be able to save the photos in JPEG or GIF format, the two formats used routinely on the Internet. Most scanner and digital camera packages accommodate all of these needs, but you should ask.

After your photo meets your satisfaction and is stored safely on your computer, it's time to transfer it to the space your ISP has provided for you on their server. Most servers require you to use an FTP program (Macs use an equivalent called Fetch) that can be downloaded as a free trial from the Internet. Sometimes your ISP will recommend an FTP program and have it available for you to download from their home page, so ask them first. If they have no specific recommendation, two of my favorites are AbsoluteFTP (**www.vandyke.com**) and CuteFTP (**www.cuteftp.com**). Basically the way all FTP programs work is to display two windows, one listing the files on your computer and the other listing the files on your ISP's server. You can move files back and forth from the server and your computer and delete files from either place, which is all you need to be an online auction photo user. FTP programs seem confusing at first, but read the HELP files supplied with them and you'll soon be on your way.

The software needs to know some address information about the server you want to connect to—I recommend you download the FTP of your choice and then call your ISP tech support to get connected. Your ISP can also tell you what URL address to type into your browser window to see your photo once it's uploaded. This will be the same address you use when filling out the online auction form to add a photo. Be sure you use capitals and lowercase EXACTLY as you see it in the filename of your photo. For instance, if you are trying to access a photo called **doll.jpg** and you type **doll.JPG** you won't find it!

If you've experimented with FTP and just can't understand exactly how to use it, ask your ISP to walk you through the process while you're sitting at your computer. They may not be familiar with the exact version of FTP you are using, but the mechanics should be very similar no matter what program they have experience with.

Using Multiple Photos with One Listing

There are times when it is necessary to display more than one photo of your item for maximum selling power. This is fairly easy to accomplish.

Instead of using the Picture URL part of the listing form, include the photos as part of the text you write for your listing information. You don't need to understand *HTML* but will need to use it to do this. HTML is hypertext markup language, which is the language of the Internet. Don't be intimidated, all you have to do is follow this example, keying in the codes exactly as here including the opening and closing brackets and slashes. We'll be selling a green Block Optic depression glass bowl and posting two photos (bowl1.jpg and bowl2.jpg) as our example. Remember: you are keying this into the description box. The different typeface in this example denotes HTML coding—you do not actually change typefaces when keying it in.

<BLOCKQUOTE>This green depression bowl in the Block Optic pattern is 8.5 inches in diameter. It is in excellent condition with no chips or cracks. Buyer pays $5.00 shipping & handling. Insurance optional. Satisfaction guaranteed.**</BLOCKQUOTE>**

<IMG SRC="http://www.yourserver.net/yourscreename/bowl1.jpg">

<IMG SRC="http://www.yourserver.net/yourscreename/bowl2.jpg">

Adding Multiple Photos on eBay™

	☐ See Item Description
Description (HTML ok)	`<blockquote>This green depression bowl in the Block Optic pattern is 8.5 inches in diameter. It is in excellent condition with no chips or cracks. Buyer pays $5.00 shipping & handling. Insurance optional. Satisfaction guaranteed.</blockquote>` `<img src=http://www.yourserver.net/yourscreename/bowl1.jpg>` `<img` (required)
Picture URL	http:// (optional)
Quantity	1 (type numerals only) (optional)
Minimum bid	7.50 per item (numerals and decimal point '.' only) (required) e.g.: 2.00
Duration	7 ▼ days (required)
Reserve price	22.50 (numerals and decimal point '.' only) (optional) e.g.: 5.00
Boldface title?	☐ ($2.00 charge) (optional)
Featured Auction?	☐ ($49.95 charge) (optional)
Featured in Category?	☐ ($9.95 charge) (optional)
Private auction?	☐ Please don't use this unless you have a specific reason. (optional)

Of course you would substitute your own description between the **<BLOCKQUOTE>** and **</BLOCKQUOTE>** codes, and the actual URL of your photos behind the **<IMG SRC=** code. Make sure you use the opening and closing quotes around the URLs. But that's it! It wasn't so hard, was it? Oh, and one more thing. When posting more than one photo, if you want to have the camera icon show up with your listing simply use the Picture URL part of the online listing form for the last photo instead of adding it in your description. In the example above, the bowl2.jpg photo would be dropped from the description and typed in the

Picture URL box. Notice that when using the Picture URL box, you do not use brackets like you do when adding photos via the description.

Should you want to add a photo to your listing after your auction is already in progress, most of the online auctions have a link called **Add To Your Item Description** or something similar. Look for it under **Seller Services** on the **Site Map**. You can add photos using the **<IMG SRC=** code exactly as it's shown in the example for adding two photos, again substituting the URL of your pictures.

Adding Multiple Photos on eBay™ to Display Camera Icon

	☐ See Item Description	
Description (HTML ok)	`<blockquote>This green depression bowl in the Block Optic pattern is 8.5 inches in diameter. It is in excellent condition with no chips or cracks. Buyer pays $5.00 shipping & handling. Insurance optional. Satisfaction guaranteed.</blockquote>` `<img src=http://www.yourserver.net/yourscreename/bowl1.jpg>`	
	(required)	
Picture URL	`http://www.yourserver.net/yourscreename/bowl2.`	
	(optional)	
Quantity	`1` (type numerals only) (optional)	
Minimum bid	`7.50` per item (numerals and decimal point '.' only) (required) *e.g.: 2.00*	
Duration	`7` days (required)	
Reserve price	`22.50` (numerals and decimal point '.' only) (optional) *e.g.: 5.00*	
Boldface title?	☐ ($2.00 charge) (optional)	
Featured Auction?	☐ ($49.95 charge) (optional)	
Featured in Category?	☐ ($9.95 charge) (optional)	
Private auction?	☐ Please don't use this unless you have a specific reason. (optional)	

Start Low

Time and time again it has been proven—you stand a much better chance of your item selling if you start the bidding low. Having no reserve will attract more bidders, as some online auction buyers just won't bid on a reserve auction. They assume that if you set a reserve it is likely high, thereby denying them a bargain.

But no reserve also leaves you open to the possibility of having to sell your item well below market value, and perhaps well below what you paid for it. If you decide to use a reserve, you should start the bidding at roughly 25% of the reserve price. This draws more bidders than if you set the opening bid high with no reserve.

Here's an example. You have an item and you won't sell it for less than $200.00. Start the bidding at $50.00 and designate a $200.00 reserve. When you start the bidding at $200.00, even if you are selling with no reserve, bidders are reluctant to begin. They might even be willing to pay your price, but would rather have a chance of getting a bargain.

This same mentality is apparent at regular auctions; if you have ever attended one you might have noticed that the auctioneer will first call a price that nobody responds to. He or she might have to drop the starting bid several times before someone will raise their hand, but once it starts the bidding almost always stops near, and often above, the first price called.

By starting low you will get the interest of more bidders who will then be "watching" your item as the auction progresses. This increases the chances of several people trying to outbid each other for your item in the closing minutes.

Getting Fancy With Your Listings

There are several software packages available that make it easy for you to create eye-catching auctions without knowing HTML. Following is an excerpt from my companion book, *The ABCs of Making Money Online* where you will find more complete reviews and information on more similar software packages.

Blackthorne Software Auction Products
(http://www.blackthornesw.com)

Blackthorne Software from Sayre, Pennsylvania has developed the definitive software package for listing and tracking your eBay™ auctions. AuctionAssistant is a well integrated group of three different programs consisting of AuctionAssistant2, which includes a great auction formatter called Ad Studio, AuctionTicker, for keeping track of your current auctions, and MegaSets, which gives you the ability to create automatic listings with selected themes. The three programs are sold separately, and AuctionAssistant2 and AuctionTicker can be used independently of each other, but all are designed to work as a group. Let's look at the features of each program individually.

AuctionAssistant2 ($59.95) is a well-designed control panel that allows you to enter your auction information, including up to three photos already stored on your computer. You can browse your hard disk for the photo you want, select it, and AuctionAssistant2 will display the correct file name and show you the actual photo(s) you have selected in a small browser window. You can then automatically upload the photo(s) to your server and post your auction to eBay™. AuctionAssistant2 then becomes a useful archival system that keeps an electronic paper trail to aid you in record keeping.

Another feature of AuctionAssistant2 is the Ad Studio, which allows you to change the colors of your type and backgrounds for your ads. Ad Studio also contains some preset "themes" that use pleasing color combinations and add music to your auctions. There are, including the default theme, a total of 20 different variations included with AuctionAssistant2 version 2.2.

AuctionTicker ($19.95) is an automated program that will log on to the Internet, search for the auction information you want to know about, and then log off. You don't even have to be in the room—your update will be waiting for you when you return. You can choose to have the information displayed in table form, as a scrolling stock-ticker-like form, or both. If you have a soundcard and speakers, you can program AuctionTicker to sound an "alarm" when an auction on your list is about to close (I use the sound of a cash register ringing to remind me it's time to check my bid and possibly bid again). It's a great way to keep from missing out on those must-have items!

MegaSet#1 ($19.95) and/or *MegaSet#2 ($19.95),* can add even more pizzazz to your auctions! While I usually don't recommend weighing your eBay™ pages down with a lot of bells and whistles, if you're inclined to do so MegaSets allows you to quickly design great ads with themesets like Patriotic, Pythonesque, or 2001 Space Odyssey. There are also holiday themesets for Valentines Day, Halloween, and Christmas. All are complete with backgrounds, colored type, and music, and the files are optimized to take up as little space as possible.

Don't Be A One-Trick Pony

It's easy to follow the crowd and use eBay™ for everything. This book teaches you how to use online auctions using eBay™ as your example, because it is simply the biggest and most well known auction site in existence. But depending on what you are selling, other sites might be better alternatives. For one thing, many other sites do not charge fees for listing items. New sites do this to attract business, and some do it simply to give them a means of competing with eBay™. You can save some listing fees by using some of the smaller sites, and you will have to determine if the prices realized are worth it or not.

Another thing to consider is that many auction sites tend to become magnets for a certain type of merchandise. If you deal in that type of merchandise you may actually do better on a site that "specializes" in it. On eBay™, the sheer mass of listings makes it hard to be noticed, and unless you have unusual items that stand out in a crowd, you're likely to be lost among the "also-rans".

Title + Description = Sales Pitch

Some people have a way with words. For those who don't, a few basic rules will get you through the writing of your auction description. This is where you put on your sales hat and convince the buying public that your merchandise is worth bidding on.

Stay away from the word "rare" in both your title and description. Rare is the most overused and abused word in the antiques and collectibles industry—most of the items described as rare are not, and items that indeed are rare are not necessarily valuable. Run a search on eBay™ for the word rare to see how many "rare" things are available for sale. Most buyers aren't drawn to listings touting merchandise as rare.

Point out flaws, but gently. Mentioning condition is important, and pointing out the flaws in an item identifies you as an honest seller. But don't dwell on the negative—start out with all of the positive aspects of your item, quickly identify flaws, and end up with more positive comments. It is an established fact that if you get too detailed about the problems of a piece, you will deflate the final bid price of that piece.

Use as many descriptive words and phrases as you can. Do some research before listing if you don't know anything about the item. Often you can find a similar item by searching the eBay™ completed auctions—you can then glean information from the descriptions of others. The more details you provide the better chance you have of attracting the bidders that will drive up the price.

CHAPTER 8
PROTECTING YOURSELF FROM INTERNET AUCTION FRAUD

A sad fact of life is that as long as online venues exist for people to buy and sell, con artists and hucksters will likely know about them. Internet auctions provide just such a venue—one that is largely unregulated. The better online auctions have taken some steps to protect your privacy and security, but when fraud occurs it comes down to the fact that you are on your own to protect yourself. Most of these sites exist simply to match buyer and seller, and the auction assumes no liability beyond that.

Online auction fraud, while not prolific, is real enough to have prompted the Federal Trade Commission to call a meeting with the top Internet auction sites in May 1998. While the cause may have been admirable, the auction representatives were not optimistic about the prospects of a successful plan to cut back on fraud. Even legally defining fraud becomes an issue; there exists a fine line between proving the seller was willfully deceiving the buyer and the buyer's failure to ask enough questions before bidding. We probably all have a different opinion of what constitutes "very good" condition, and other such generic terms. As with transactions you make in your everyday life the common sense approach seems to be "buyer beware."

While there is no fail-safe way to be sure you're dealing with a reputable buyer or seller, there are some steps you can take to greatly reduce your risk.

BUYERS' REMEDIES

√ Read the Description Twice

Reading a description the first time through most people will have a mental image of the item, as they would like it to be. The second time reality begins to set in. And for some of us it takes a third and fourth read before we really get the picture. The extra time is worth it—the most common complaint from online auction buyers is that the merchandise was not as described. This can also mean the buyer did not interpret the description as the seller intended.

√ E-mail Sellers with Questions

Descriptions of merchandise being sold via online auctions vary from highly detailed to unbelievably incoherent. Even the highly detailed ones probably won't answer every question you should ask the seller. Clarifications on condition, color, manufacturer's marks and size or dimensions are sometimes necessary—although photos are an extremely important aid to the description they can be deceiving. More importantly, two questions that are almost never answered in the description should be the first ones you ask: sellers return policy (covered next) and shipping charges. Almost invariably the seller will mention in the description "Buyer pays shipping," which is normal and fair for online auctions. But how much shipping? Some will send your package for the actual cost of postage. Others charge a handling fee and I've seen them range from $0.25 to $5.00 for handling on a small object alone. Sellers are entitled to a handling fee to cover expenses of packing materials and their time. But some are using the handling fee as a profit extender and you should know before you buy how much you'll be charged. If it seems exorbitant, don't bid.

√ Know the Seller's Return Policy

Make sure you understand the seller's return policy, especially if you're bidding on a high-ticket item. Most don't mention their policy so be sure to inquire before you bid. Buyers remorse is never an excuse to return an item, but if you feel strongly that the merchandise is not what was described you should know your options.

I've seen sellers who absolutely refuse to accept returned items. Some charge restocking fees designed to make it cost-prohibitive to return things, and some will honor *legitimate* returns as long as you are willing to pay their cost of running that particular auction and/or shipping charges to return the item. My advice is simply this: *don't bid on an auction where the seller has a no return policy*. I don't buy from antique malls or retailers advertising a no return policy and online sellers are no different.

√ Insure Your Purchases

Still another consideration is whether or not the item will be insured; some sellers require you to pay for insurance while others let you decide or never mention it at all. Any item you are willing to pay your hard-earned money for is worth insuring, especially breakables. Requesting insurance lets the seller know you are a serious buyer and as such won't be as quick to tolerate inferior merchandise or service. In my dealings with shipping online auction merchandise I have not had a single package lost in the mail in over 300 shipments; however there has been breakage reported eight times. I deal primarily with the U.S. Postal Service and except for one case all claims have been fully paid promptly and courteously. The one "problem" case involved a buyer living on a U.S. military installation. The buyer was asked to fill out forms that were then mailed to the seller (me). I had to fill out the seller's part and mail them somewhere else for verification. Sadly the buyer e-mailed me two months after I had returned the forms to let me know they still had not heard a thing about their claim. I don't know if the difference in the refund procedure was due to the APO address or not, but it may be something buyers living on military bases should be aware of.

The U.S. Postal Service charges a small fee for insurance which is well worth the expense; you will find this schedule of fees in Appendix B. UPS will insure packages with a declared valued up to $100.00 for no extra charge. Higher amounts can be purchased at a cost of $0.35 for each $100.00 of declared value over $100.00, with a maximum of $50,000. Federal Express also gives you the first $100.00 of declared value at no extra charge, and then charges a minimum of $2.50 for insurance up to $500.00. Above that the charge is $0.50 for each $100.00 increment or fraction thereof.

√ Can You See It?

Photos of merchandise being offered are common when using the larger online auctions and infinitely helpful in making buying decisions. How often have you bought something from a retail store or catalog without seeing at least a picture? Most of you wouldn't do such a thing, and you shouldn't buy something online unless there is a photo of it posted.

Some sellers don't post a photo but offer to e-mail one if you request it. This is fine, and you should by all means request the photo if you're interested in what they have to offer. Once you've seen it you know it exists, and many of us are better equipped to make decisions based on sight rather than reading a description.

There are enough options available to today's online sellers—ranging from low-cost digital cameras and scanners to photo studios that can convert images to Internet formats—that there just isn't an excuse for not having a photo available for a prospective buyer. For information on how to post your pictures once you have them digitized, see chapter 7—Advanced Tips for Online Auction Users.

√ Read the Feedback

Most online auctions provide the ability for registered auction-goers to leave feedback for buyers or sellers they've had dealings with. You can leave positive, negative, or neutral comments and the results are posted and available to anyone requesting the information. Before bidding on merchandise from a seller you aren't familiar with, read their feedback profile. There should be few, if any, negative comments.

If there are one or two negatives posted, e-mail the person(s) who left them (e-mail addresses are usually available with the feedback summary) and ask for details. Most online auction users are happy to talk about their experiences, good or bad. Don't rule out someone with a negative or two if there are many positives—perhaps the comment was unfair or unwarranted or the matter could have been amicably resolved had the offended party been more patient.

√ Return When Not As Described

When you accept merchandise that is not what the seller described, you are contributing to the stereotype of antique dealers being dishonest. My personal experiences, both online and off, is that the vast majority of antique and collectible dealers are honest and concerned about the reputation of the industry. If you find one that isn't, letting them get away with it encourages unacceptable behavior.

Since you've already determined you are dealing with someone having an acceptable return policy (you have done that, haven't you?), by returning the item you're saying, "I don't accept inferior merchandise." Of course, reread the description before contacting the seller and make sure your expectations weren't too high. If they were, accept your mistake and leave positive feedback for the seller. If you're still sure you didn't get what was described, make contact and explain your reasons for the return.

√ Add Your 2 Cents

It's been mentioned before but it's worth mentioning again: after completing your transactions, make sure you post feedback about the other party. Don't be shy if you've been ripped off—some people won't post negative feedback about someone else for fear of retaliation and receiving negative feedback themselves. While this can't be ruled out, astute online auction users know that some negatives are unwarranted and won't hold them against you, especially when the vast majority of your feedback is glowing. An undeserved negative may hurt your pride, but you've done the auction community a service by exposing a con artist. And leaving feedback is like voting: if you don't do it you have no reason to complain when the system doesn't suit you.

√ Visit Chat Rooms

Some of the online auctions have chat rooms where buyers and sellers gather to talk about their experiences. You can gain valuable auction tips here as well as learn about particular users who have abused the system.

SELLERS' REMEDIES

√ Nonpayment

Buyer's remorse is a part of this business you'll probably have to deal with at some point if you sell long enough. Be sure you make every effort to solve the situation amicably first but when the buyer doesn't pay up and offers no reasons after two weeks, post negative feedback. The fee to list your item is probably nonrefundable, but many of the online auctions will credit your account for the commission charge if you ask. Make sure you ask. And add this buyer to your no-repeat-business list.

√ Item Switching

A few unscrupulous buyers are upgrading their collections by making a purchase, claiming a defect with the merchandise, and returning an identical item of lesser quality, sometimes even damaged. The only way I can suggest to combat this scam is to photograph your item before you ship it and store the photo with documentation about the condition. Of course I wouldn't do it for everything, but you know which pieces you need to protect.

BENEFICIAL TO BOTH BUYER AND SELLER

√ Escrow Companies

Many of the online auctions are beginning to promote the services of a third party Escrow Company to act as a go-between for buyer and seller. The escrow companies benefit both parties—buyers are protected from fraudulent merchandise and sellers get protection from buyers who don't pay. Money from the buyer is sent to the Escrow Company, who holds it in trust until the merchandise is delivered and accepted. The Escrow Company then releases the buyer's funds to the seller. Should the merchandise not be as described or never delivered, the money is not yet in the sellers hands. Conversely, if the buyer does not pay, the seller never has to ship the merchandise.

√ Online Help

eBay™ has an area of their community set aside for help and protection with online transactions. It is called SafeHarbor™ and includes links to the eBay™ help desk, the tutorial, an Escrow Company, and other useful information.

Information from other sources is also available online about protecting yourself from fraud when using the Internet. The Federal Trade Commission maintains a site **(www.ftc.gov)** with consumer information that applies to Internet shopping in general, not just auctions. From their home page click on <u>Consumer Protection</u> and then on <u>E-commerce and the Internet</u> for a list of topics.

If you follow the recommendations outlined in this chapter and still become a victim of fraud, you do have other options. The National Fraud Information Center in March of 1996 launched the Internet Fraud Watch, enabling them to expand their responsibilities to this area of commerce. Electronic forms are available to report fraudulent practices or request information. You can reach the Internet Fraud Watch at **www.fraud.org** or by calling **1-800-876-7060**.

If you buy from a business and get ripped off, you can go to **www.bbb.org** and also file a complaint with the Better Business Bureau. You might as well make noise with as many third party enforcement organizations as you can—after all, it's your money!

Lace, ribbons and embroidery pieces with a cigarette silk (advertising Red Sun cigarettes on the back) of Hope Latham.

A pieced quilt in red, white and blue.

An oak kitchen clock from the late 19th century.

Pikachu is the most popular "pocket monster" of all the Pokemons.

CHAPTER 9
NOW EVERYONE CAN ACCEPT
CREDIT CARDS

Until September of 1999, accepting credit cards for most of us was no easy task. If you were lucky enough to qualify for a merchant account from a bank, the paperwork and expense involved in accepting credit cards made it nearly impossible for home business owners, hobbyists, and even some small businesses to consider it.

Let's say you are a seller using an online auction, or a collector wanting to sell some of your early acquisitions that you have since replaced with examples in better condition. You've read *The ABCs of Making Money Online* and have designed your own Web site storefront, and you know that the convenience of being able to accept credit cards will open your inventory to customers who otherwise might not be willing to bid or place an order. In addition, you know that the psychology behind a prospective buyer's top price is how much cash they have on hand, and they will often go higher if they know they can pay with plastic. Accepting credit cards would be a big plus for your business, but the costs and fees have kept you from taking advantage.

Enter **PayPal** *(http://www.paypal.com),* a free person-to-person payment service from **X.com** with an ingenious, safe, secure, way to transfer funds to anyone with an e-mail address. What does this have to do with accepting credit cards? Plenty. Here's how PayPal works.

You register with PayPal (go ahead, it's free!) and while you do not have to place a credit card on file with them I recommend that you do. That way when you need to send money to someone else and your account balance is less than you owe, the remainder can be painlessly charged to your credit card, giving you as much as a month to raise the extra cash and pay the balance due off when your statement arrives.

Read that last sentence again. As simple as it sounds, when sending money through PayPal you can use your credit card to pay for auctions you win, items you purchase, and even send your college student son or daughter money. Money you owe to any person for any reason can be sent with PayPal and charged to your credit card. Best of all, it's completely free and the money you send is treated as a purchase, not a cash

http://www.paypal.com

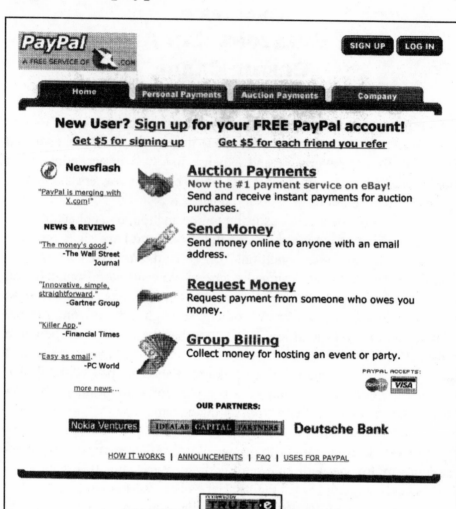

PayPal
A FREE SERVICE OF X .COM

SIGN UP   LOG IN

Home   Personal Payments   Auction Payments   Company

New User? <u>Sign up</u> for your FREE PayPal account!
<u>Get $5 for signing up</u>   <u>Get $5 for each friend you refer</u>

Newsflash

"<u>PayPal is merging with X.com</u>!"

NEWS & REVIEWS

"<u>The money's good</u>."
-The Wall Street Journal

"<u>Innovative, simple, straightforward</u>."
-Gartner Group

"<u>Killer App</u>."
-Financial Times

"<u>Easy as email</u>."
-PC World

<u>more news</u>...

Auction Payments
Now the #1 payment service on eBay!
Send and receive instant payments for auction purchases.

Send Money
Send money online to anyone with an email address.

Request Money
Request payment from someone who owes you money.

Group Billing
Collect money for hosting an event or party.

PAYPAL ACCEPTS:
VISA

OUR PARTNERS:

Nokia Ventures   IDEALAB CAPITAL PARTNERS   **Deutsche Bank**

<u>HOW IT WORKS</u> | <u>ANNOUNCEMENTS</u> | <u>FAQ</u> | <u>USES FOR PAYPAL</u>

advance. With most credit cards this means a 25-day grace period before interest accrues.

Of course this also means that people who purchase from you can use their credit cards to pay, without you needing a merchant account. The money they send you is instantly credited to your account, and you have the option of leaving it there to be used to pay for items you purchase, having PayPal send you a check, or you can even have it electronically transferred to your bank account. There is no waiting for a check to clear as PayPal payments clear as soon as they are sent. Sellers should treat PayPal payments like cash, and ship merchandise as soon as they are received.

Some of you are probably thinking that you really don't like giving your credit card information out online, and with PayPal you don't have to. Instead of using a credit card you can send PayPal a check to deposit into your account, giving you a balance to work with. If you use PayPal only to accept payments there is also no need to register a credit card. But the fact is that at this point in time doing business on the Internet is more convenient using plastic, and some sites require you to register one before allowing you certain privileges. PayPal credit card information is taken on a secure server, making it as safe as the Internet allows.

How does PayPal do all of this and still keep it free for all of us? The answer is as ingenious and simple as the rest of their service—they count on most of us to leave balances in our accounts. The money we leave riding in our accounts resides in a safe money market mutual fund, with the interest acting as an income stream to keep PayPal alive and well. Each of us, therefore, can participate in keeping PayPal free for everyone by using our accounts as a holding tank for the money deposited there. Most of us buy as much or more as we sell anyway, and by maintaining a balance the money will be there to pay for our purchases.

eBay realized that PayPal was on to something, and quickly developed their own version of sending online payments. However **Billpoint** falls well short of the benefits of using PayPal, with the biggest difference being that Billpoint charges for their service. Following is the text from the Billpoint site explaining their reasons for charging fees...

"Yes, there is a fee to sellers for use of the Billpoint online payments service.

Providing a service that enables eBay buyers and sellers to pay each other through online credit card payments is very different from the services currently provided on eBay. There are significant costs associated with administering credit card payments. These costs include the fees charged by credit card associations such as Visa, Mastercard, and Discover for participation in their programs, payment processing costs, and back office operational costs. Consequently, Billpoint must charge a fee based upon use of the service.

Billpoint has different pricing packages which vary based upon a sellers' payment needs, sales volume, history on eBay, and eBay account status. In general, fees range from $0.35 + 3.5% per transaction to $0.55 + 5.5% per transaction based on the total amount of the payment. Billpoint charges a flat fee ranging from $0.35 to $0.55 for payments of $10.00 and less. Billpoint only charges a fee if the buyer pays for the item using Billpoint online payments. Billpoint fees are automatically deducted from your upcoming deposits. There are no set-up fees, no monthly fees, and no minimum charge requirements.

Please note that your Billpoint fees are in addition to and separate from your eBay fees."

No matter how you read this, it means paying for a service that is provided free of charge by PayPal. PayPal has evolved into one of the most exciting new business opportunities available to the average consumer, and I strongly urge you to visit the site and learn more. In the future, PayPal plans to offer their service on Web-enabled cell phones, pagers, and other handheld devices, as well as offer support for international users sometime during the year 2000.

A "Falcon Ware" water pitcher made in England.

Four china "pin cushion" dolls were used as decoration on lamps, brushes, and other objects as well as pincushions, in the early 20th century.

A decorative figural lamp "The Hunter" with a rose and green colored glass shade.

Satin glass boudoir lamps in blue, pink, and green. *Photo courtesy Sharon Merwin.*

EPILOGUE
BUYER BEWARE!

Although you are exposed to hundreds, perhaps thousands, of objects to collect on the Net, the variety is counterbalanced by the possibility that the items aren't necessarily described in the terms and with the accuracy you would wish. This may be because the person selling the item is not knowledgeable about this particular kind of collectible. When you see terms misused, it should be a signal to you to inquire further about the object.

Another warning signal is when the photograph of the object you are interested in is too fuzzy to clearly show details. Perhaps the seller is just a bad photographer, but unless you can clearly see the item in the photograph, it is wise to steer clear or at least request another picture before bidding.

It is not at all unusual for an item to be listed in the wrong category. "Antique Dolls" is a category that covers a lot of territory, but dolls like a 1967 Eegee doll, a *Crissy* doll, or a Precious Moments nativity set, all of which are listed as "antiques" as this is written, do not belong in that category!

As a doll collector, I am often puzzled and sometimes amused at the descriptions given for dolls. At the moment a 15in (38cm) "German Schoenhut Doll" is listed with references to Jan Foulke's *Blue Book* and Coleman's *Collector's Encyclopedia of Dolls*. How would someone with access to those two excellent reference books make such a basic mistake as to call a Schoenhut a German doll? Right away that seller loses credibility.

I am always wary of the term "rare" used in a description. Perhaps this is just a way to entice buyers to look at a particular selection, but it is misused in the vast majority of cases. "Very rare," "very old," and "early" are also often misused. As this is written there is a "Rare German paper (sic) mache, ca 1880" listed. It appears to be a nice doll, but rare she is not! An "Early 1800's Wax Doll—Rare" is also interesting, but the photograph indicates that she is a wax-over composition with pierced ears that dates from the last quarter of the 19th century, so I have a problem with the use of both "rare" and "early" in that description.

One listing I remember was a doll advertised as a "bisque head" "Holtzmasse." Curious because it could only be one or the other but not both, I found out that it was a bisque head doll by Cuno & Otto Dressel—the firm that held the trademark for "Holtzmasse." Holtzmasse is a word for a wood-pulp composition material so it was stamped on their papier-mâché dolls but never on their bisque ones. So it is still a puzzle—"Holtzmasse" is nowhere on the doll (nor should it be) but indicates some knowledge of the COD dolls. However, why would a seller pick up that term "out of the air" and use (or misuse) it to describe a bisque doll?

Carolyn Cook

APPENDIX A
GLOSSARY

Alta Vista—one of the major search engines on the World Wide Web.

America Online—an online community of member services and gateway to the Internet.

auction frenzy—the madness that sometimes prevails in the last few minutes of an online auction as bidders try to outbid each other.

bookmarking—storing the Internet addresses of your favorite Web sites for fast retrieval later.

browser—software that enables your computer to translate and display Web pages on your computer monitor.

CD ROM—Compact Disk, Read Only Memory. The disk looks like a typical music CD and holds data to install programs or run games on your computer.

clicking—the act of pressing one of the buttons on your computer mouse.

Control Panel—an area of your computer accessible from the Start—Settings menu.

copy & paste—two separate functions that allows you to make a copy of some data and place it in another file. Usually found under the Edit menu of your word processing program.

crop—electronically "trimming away" any extraneous parts of a photograph, leaving only as much of the image as is necessary to show off your item. The photo manipulation software that comes with most scanners or digital cameras allows you to do this.

Earthlink—a national Internet Service Provider.

encryption—a method of "coding" information sent via e-mail to make it much more difficult for anyone, other than the recipient, to be able to intercept and interpret it.

flaming—the online equivalent of vehemently criticizing someone, sometimes nastily.

frames—a construction technique used by some Web site designers that utilizes two or more windows open at the same time. Some older browsers cannot interpret frames.

FTP—file transfer protocol. Software that enables you to move files between your ISP's server and your computer.

http—hypertext transfer protocol. The rules used to create Web pages, enabling users to transfer hypertext and multimedia from one networked computer to another.

hyperlink—word(s) or photo(s) on a Web page that, when clicked, take you to another area of the World Wide Web.

iMac—the first new computer introduction by Macintosh in years. Designed to compete with the PC in the under $1,500.00 consumer computer market.

ISDN—Integrated Services Digital Network. A series of standards for transmission over ordinary telephone lines at up to 128 Kbps. Typically costs $400–$500 for installation and $20 monthly over and above your regular phone charges.

ISP—Internet Service Provider. A business that provides Internet access to the public.

Keywords—descriptive word(s) and phrases used to instruct other software, often search engines, to perform certain tasks.

Launch—the act of initiating a program on your computer.

Linking—the ability, through the use of hypertext transfer protocol, to move from one part of the World Wide Web to another.

Macintosh—a computer that competes with the PC and runs a completely different operating system.

megahertz—a unit of measurement (one million cycles of electromagnetic currency alternation per second) used to rate the speed of computer microprocessors. The higher the megahertz rating, the faster the computer microprocessor can interpret information.

Modem—Hardware that enables two networked computers to transfer data back and forth.

newsgroup—an online group formed to discuss one particular topic.

PC—Personal Computer. IBM built the first PCs but today the market is dominated by PC clones built by other manufacturers.

Point your browser—instructing your browser software as to its next destination.

RAM—Random Access Memory. Hardware that stores important data for running your computer. The more RAM your computer has the faster most applications will run.

reserve—the minimum amount of money you are willing to accept for your item.

robot—a program that automatically scans the Web and retrieves HTML documents to be indexed and stored for later retrieval.

Search engine—a powerful program that enables you to locate specific information on the World Wide Web by typing in descriptive words.

sniper—an online auction participant who waits until the last minutes of an online auction and then places a high bid with little time left for others to outbid them.

sniping—the act of waiting until the last minutes of an online auction to place your bid with the intent of leaving other bidders no time to outbid you.

Storefront Auction—an online auction that is actually a retail Web site in disguise.

T-1 Line—a direct connection to the Internet using fiber optic cabling with speeds of up to 192 Kbps.

URL—Uniform Resource Locator. An Internet address that you type in to access a Web page. Each Web page has a unique URL so that it can be individually accessed by anyone online.

Usenet—newsgroups when referred to collectively rather than individually.

Web page—all of the text, graphics, audio and video that your browser displays when you type in an Internet address, or URL.

Web site—a series of Web pages on a common topic that are linked together using hyperlinks.

WebTV—a device, similar in appearance to a cable TV box, that enables the user to connect to the Internet without a computer.

Yahoo—one of the major search engines on the World Wide Web.

APPENDIX B
U.S. POSTAL SERVICE RATE CHARTS

These rates are taken from the U.S. Postal Service Web site (**www.usps.gov**) and reflect current rates that went into effect January 10, 1999.

Priority Mail

Up to 2 pounds	$3.20
Up to 3 pounds	$4.30
Up to 4 pounds	$5.40
Up to 5 pounds	$6.50

Over 5 pounds the rates change according to distance shipped. For best accuracy take packed item to your local post office with the zip code of recipient, or visit **www.usps.gov** to calculate cost.

First-Class Mail

1 ounce	$0.33
2 ounces	$0.55
3 ounces	$0.77
4 ounces	$0.99
5 ounces	$1.21
6 ounces	$1.43
7 ounces	$1.65
8 ounces	$1.87
9 ounces	$2.09
10 ounces	$2.31
11 ounces	$2.53
12 ounces	$2.75
13 ounces	$2.97

Over 13 ounces see Priority Mail

Insurance

Coverage is based on amount of insured value. Do not insure a package for more than its value.

Insured Value	Fee
$0.01-$50.00	$085
$50.00-$100.00	$1.80
$100.01-$200.00	$2.75
$200.01-$300.00	$3.70
$300.01-$400.00	$4.65
$400.01-$500.00	$5.60
$500.01-$600.00	$6.55
$600.01-$700.00	$7.50
$700.01-$800.00	$8.45
$800.01-$900.00	$9.40
$900.01-$1,000.00	$10.35
$1,000.01-$5,000.00	$10.35

Additional insurance is $0.95 for each $100.00 or fraction thereof over $1,000.00.

Insured mail maximum liability: $5,000.00.

ABOUT THE AUTHOR

Ray Boileau has been involved in the pre-press and printing industry for twenty-five years and was among the first in the 1970s to experiment with computers as a complement to printing, long before desktop publishing was conceived. He currently is a computer consultant who designs Web pages and specializes in Web site implementation.

Ray has also been buying and selling antiques and collectibles for eighteen years. He now works as an antiques dealer offering Internet sales as well as selling through several conventional locations. He has been using or monitoring many of the online auctions since their inceptions.

INDEX